THE REFORM
OF POWER

A Proposal for
an International Security System

LEONARD BEATON

With a Foreword by
The Right Honourable Lester B. Pearson

The Viking Press | *New York*

Published in 1972 by The Viking Press, Inc.
625 Madison Avenue, New York, N.Y. 10022
Published simultaneously in Canada by
The Macmillan Company of Canada Limited
SBN 670-59304-4
Library of Congress catalog card number: 76-171895
Printed in U.S.A.

PREFACE

This book was begun in 1965, when I was on the staff of the Institute for Strategic Studies, London, and the original draft was written for a joint study group sponsored by I.S.S. and the Royal Institute of International Affairs. The Tocqueville Project subsequently sponsored a study on the politics of arms control which forms part of the central section of the book. A visiting chair at Carleton University, Ottawa, in 1970 provided the opportunity to rewrite the manuscript. I owe a debt to each of these organizations and also to those who have been willing to read and comment on the argument at various stages of its development.

Leonard Beaton
London,
March, 1971

FOREWORD

BY

THE RIGHT HONOURABLE

LESTER B. PEARSON

LEONARD BEATON's last book can only increase our sense of great loss at his premature and lamented death. In it he leaves us an important legacy of constructive ideas and proposals on the vitally important subject with which he deals, "The Reform of Power".

Reform of power can only be brought about by a reform of policy leading to a better understanding, especially by the "Super-powers", of the relationship between power for national defence and power for global destruction; between the inescapable compulsion of interdependence and the pressures of independence.

Beaton rejects as impossible, and even undesirable, the idea that any international structure should be based on world government; or that sovereign states should be required to give up national responsibility for national defence. Instead he would add to this responsibility "commitments and assignments" for international security after the N.A.T.O. pattern, which would bring about a synthesis of national and international policy and supra-national force in the interest of the kind of security which alone can ensure survival.

In seeking this, Beaton believes that we must move forward from the present, step by step, using the international institutions we now have, while creating new ones for specific tasks when needed and as possible. To this end, governments must identify and develop "a common security interest below the level of actual political dispute" (p. 167).

Beaton sees evidence of progress in this search for such a common interest in the nuclear arms talks on testing, non-

3

proliferation and control; in the growing awareness of the danger from the commitment of great powers to opposite sides in conflict between smaller powers; in the increase of functional co-operation in new fields where the interdependence is obvious.

It is not easy to be optimistic on this score. It is easier to agree with Beaton that any such evolution will require immense political wisdom and effort, cannot be based on any central monopoly of power, and will be determined largely by relations between the Super-powers and, particularly, on their success in dealing with the menace of nuclear arms.

If progress is bound to be slow and hesitant, will there be time for the fundamental changes in international thinking and national policy which are necessary for enduring peace? Leonard Beaton thinks so, because he believes that the world today with all its dangers appears much more secure than anyone believed possible when the cold war was raging twenty years ago.

I hope he is right, but I cannot, myself, find as much hope and comfort as I would like from this improvement. It is largely due to the acceptance by the Super-powers of a balance of nuclear deterrence which can be too easily disturbed.

Leonard Beaton moves among these awesome problems of international security with impressive knowledge, cool wisdom and deep understanding. As a result, we have in *The Reform of Power* a book of very real importance which should be widely read.

CONTENTS

THE REFORM OF POWER

1

INTERNATIONAL SECURITY

ALL governments seek security for their country and people. Keeping out the invader and maintaining the civil peace are the first duties of those who hold political power. If challenged, most peoples are prepared to sacrifice much of their wealth and many lives to protect their security as they understand it. Armed forces are permanently maintained in case some external or internal menace may develop and to sustain broader arrangements which are thought to keep the country safe. Security was the original business of monarchs and rulers and it remains fundamental to modern governments.

For states, as for individuals, security can seldom be an absolute condition. Most people who live in orderly societies would consider that they had reasonable personal safety: yet they are subject to the perils of personal accident, earthquakes or drunken drivers. All that they can ask of their society, and all that they generally expect, is a reasonable prospect of survival and a high probability of living the sort of life they choose. The same can be said of states. They do not seek some absolute level of security through the arrangements they normally make – armaments, military forces in being, alliances, international institutions. They seek what they calculate will be a reasonable likelihood that they can design and operate their own institutions in their own territory. Governments generally want to preserve their monopoly or near-monopoly of force over a defined area against any long-term or short-term threats from inside or outside. They may become convinced of the importance of certain friendly governments to their security or the need to prevent others from acquiring weapons or raising forces to a level they find threatening. Strong powers also tend to construct security policies on wider assumptions: that, for example, strategic areas should be kept friendly. They may also react to a change in the military posture or sympathies of a rival or neighbour. It can be argued that Germany went to war in 1914 because her strategic theory compelled her to do so in the face of Russian mobilization. More recently, a President of the United States could state* that "nuclear weapons are so destructive, and ballistic missiles are so swift, that any substantially increased possibility of their use or any sudden change in their deployment may well be regarded as a definite threat to the peace".

The anxiety to achieve a safer system of power in the world —an effective international order—has been prominent for many years and particularly since the full horror of nuclear arms was demonstrated beyond doubt. The emergence of weapons of such destructive power has convinced many people that a security system built on sovereign governments is too prone to break down to be sustained for long. Others console themselves with the hope that the use of nuclear and thermonuclear weapons is and will be so intolerable that it becomes all but impossible: and this, they feel, will also rule out any action which might lead by sure steps to the employment of these weapons. In all the significant powers, these essentially radical and conservative schools of opinion have had a long debate about the best system of security. Most governments make a place for both in their policy: they build their security on national or alliance foundations; and they proclaim that this is temporary and inadequate and that the security of the future must be based on disarmament and a new international order.

These two positions are usually seen as opposites and those favouring one commonly mistrust the other—the hard line and the soft line, the tough nationalists and the complaisant internationalists, the pessimists and the optimists. But it can be argued that they are opposed in their means and not their ends. For the end of each is security. The central objec-

* This statement was made by President Kennedy in October, 1962, in explanation of his decision to impose a quarantine on the movement of Soviet ships to Cuba.

tion of the internationalists to the world system as it is now operating is that it cannot provide security. Though it is less often stated in so many words, this is also the main objection of the nationalists to disarmament plans. Each side has its case. Those who look to world institutions to operate a system of international security seldom speculate on the security problems this would create if it was achieved; and those who put their faith in the present order tend to ignore the problems which technology, political change, nuclear proliferation and miscalculation are increasingly loading on to it.

This study is an attempt to cut across the traditional lines of the argument and to examine a new approach. To those who are committed to one side or the other of an established debate, the suggestion that the issue has been wrongly defined is inevitably tiresome. The protagonists are inclined to suspect an attempt to avoid the unacceptable consequences of either course by having it both ways. This study must be open to such criticism. It accepts the orthodox propositions that invulnerable nuclear weapons have served the peace and that to expect the present security system to be abandoned by the main powers is to delude oneself; and it also accepts the radical propositions that there are constant risks of a crisis in which control might be lost and longer term challenges of a fundamental kind which make it necessary to develop international security institutions. To the charge that this is trying to have it both ways, it can only be replied that we must have it both ways, that either one or the other is inadequate. But the thesis argued here is that there is no basic inconsistency and that certain elements of artifice are normal and essential in the art of politics.

In western speculation, what might be considered the great tradition of international security is associated with the moral and legal traditions of natural law and looks to Grotius as its classic figure. This tradition, in effect, lays down standards for the conduct of states and judges them in relation to these standards. With this is associated the notion of the just and the unjust war—theories which flourished, incidentally, as Martin Wight has pointed out,* in two centuries of "violent and unscrupulous" diplomacy from the mid-seventeenth to the mid-nineteenth centuries. A second tradition, the positivist, is also strongly established. It recognizes limits on the actions of states but only on the basis of their own formal consent. International law and practice thus become codified in the various instruments of the states system. Wight observes that this prevailing tone in nineteenth century theory was once more in contrast with the international life of the age.† "It is curious that a theory which starts from the axiom of a legal self-sufficiency . . . should have flourished in an age when the conception of Europe as a cultural and moral community acquired a new vigour, and the diplomatic system of the Concert maintained standards of good faith, mutual consideration and restraint higher probably than at any other time in international history". He finds a deeper theory among the practitioners than among the theoreticians and lawyers. A protocol to the London Conference on Belgium of 1831 reads: "Chaque Nation a ses droits particuliers; mais l'Europe aussi a son droit; c'est l'ordre social qui le lui a donné."

It is this view which underlies the approach of this study. Each nation has its own security policy and its own interests. But the world as a whole has interests: and as in any larger political entity constructed from lesser but self-conscious units, the general interest supports some elements of each particular interest and opposes or confines others. Hedley Bull has stated the challenge which faces us:‡ "The idea of international society . . . is the idea with which a new analysis of the problem of international relations should now begin." Martin Wight has added the implications:§

* *Diplomatic Investigations*, ed. Herbert Butterfield and Martin Wight (London, Allen and Unwin), p. 29. Wight's essays in this small volume constitute what is perhaps the most profound and perceptive introduction to the notion of international society in our time.

† Ibid., p. 30.

‡ "The Twenty Years Crisis Thirty Years On", *International Journal*, vol. XXIV, no. 4, Autumn, 1969, p. 638.

§ Op. cit., p. 103.

"If there is an international society, then there is an order of some kind to be maintained, or even developed. It is not fallacious to speak of a collective interest, and security acquires a broadened meaning: it can be enjoyed or pursued in common. Foreign policy will take some account of the common interest. It becomes possible to transfer to international politics some of the categories of constitutionalism."

States vary in their attitudes to international society depending on their position and size, and their relationship to those who appear predominant. Large powers are inevitably involved in the definition and maintenance of whatever order is functioning. Small states sometimes feel a sense of participation from the working of their sympathies or alignments, or from their part in international institutions; more commonly, however, they feel a detachment born of impotence. Whatever their part in things, there are very few states which are not conscious of their interest in a secure international order. Virtually all recognize the need to avoid a situation in which there might be war or violence on any important scale. If armed conflict occurs, there is a general interest in preventing the use of weapons of mass destruction and in keeping the fighting limited in area. War is so unpredictable and has proved so often to be controlled less by reason and interest than by its own laws that even without nuclear weapons it has always been a special source of insecurity. Even in the absence of warfare or of visibly aggressor states, insecurity is feared from technological evolution and the development of new weapons.

While it may be widely accepted that there is an international security interest, there is little agreement about how it is to be discovered and implemented. This rather than the proper way to embark on disarmament or arms control is surely the central question in the reform of power. The discovery of appropriate solutions may well be impeded by false analogies about how an international order ought to develop. Western speculation, in particular, is powerfully influenced by the national state analogy, a tradition which is due in part to the predominance of lawyers in the study of international organization.* The general western legal view of the national state is that a monopoly of power is held under a single authority; that the proof of that monopoly is that no individual or group can challenge it; and that the institutions of the state make and enforce the laws in the common interest. It is inherent in the construction of a coherent legal system that fictions must be employed: and many of those concerned with the real government of states are well aware that this image of the national state is fictional. In fact, the institutions seldom rest on genuine monopoly of real power, even if in most cases they rest on a single military force under unified command. A consensus is constantly being built from diverse elements and a failure to sustain this process will lead to the break-up of the state or to drastic alterations in its government. But even if the legal image of the national state was valid, its extension to international society would obscure certain enduring realities. The notion of the monopoly of power cannot be extended to any conceivable world order. Yet as an end point, as an ultimate objective, it is immensely influential. The United States proposals for general and complete disarmament of 1962 (these will be discussed in detail in Chapter 3) strengthen the United Nations Peace Force "until it had sufficient armed forces and armaments so that no state could challenge it". When it is considered what armed forces and armaments the United States has and the challenge to these which has been mounted by the half-state of the Vietcong supported by North Vietnam, it is possible to form some conception of the forces a world authority would need so that the United States or the Soviet Union could not challenge it. Equally, the British Government criticizes the Soviet proposals for general disarmament in these words.† "Reductions on the

* Perhaps the purest contemporary version of this is *World Peace Through World Law*, by Grenville Clark and Louis B. Sohn (Harvard U.P. (3rd edition), 1966). The four volumes of *The Strategy of World Order*, by Richard A. Falk and Saul H. Mendlovitz (World Law Fund, New York, 1966), were built on the Clark–Sohn thesis.

† *Disarmament: the Path to Peace* (H.M.S.O., 1968), paragraph 16. The italics have been inserted.

scale proposed could be made only when confidence in the disarmament process had been fully established, reliable verification procedures were in force, and *an effective international peacekeeping force had been set up.*" Dr. Herman Kahn* has listed six possibilities which might produce what he calls an international agency with a near-monopoly of force. He considers it "quite possible that even a 'bad' world government is preferable to an accelerated and uncontrolled arms race". These sentiments are widely held; and the feeling that there is a solution (however costly it might prove) in the notion of government can be held to be part of the western view of international society.

The conflict of what might be called western legal ideology and political practice emerged with useful clarity in the critical debate between Mr. Dean Acheson and Mr. Bernard Baruch in 1946 over American policy on the future organization of atomic energy. The United States was proposing an international system to control this new technology and to prevent it from being used for weapons purposes. The great question was what would happen if at some future date a state rejected its undertakings to the system. Baruch's position was summarized by the official historians of the U.S. Atomic Energy Commission† in these words: "It was important to show the necessity of enforcing the engagements of the nations. Baruch considered the penalties the *sine qua non.* He was quite aware that this might bring the United Nations 'athwart of the veto power', for war, the ultimate penalty, might be necessary." This passage illustrates in relation to a single subject what is implied in the general notion of a central legal authority. To create and maintain an effective centre of power means introducing world war itself—for that is what is involved with a great power—as a means of sustaining a system designed to abolish war. Had the Baruch Plan been adopted, and had the Soviet

* In "Daedalus", the *Journal of the American Academy of Arts & Sciences,* Fall, 1960, p. 780.

† "The New World", vol. 1 of the *History of the U.S. Atomic Energy Commission,* by Richard G. Hewlett and Oscar E. Anderson (Pennsylvania State U.P., 1962), p. 573.

Government later decided to equip itself with nuclear weapons, a significant and very honourable sector of western opinion would undoubtedly have considered that the future of the world depended on meeting the challenge with enforcements and so with world war. The proposition reduces itself rapidly to absurdity. Lincoln's America may have shown that it was one nation indivisible, but we are and must remain one world divisible.

Mr. Dean Acheson's critique of Baruch went to the heart of the problem and expounded the effective rather than the ideological western position. He argued* that "if safeguards failed or the international situation collapsed, each nation had to be left in a relatively secure position". In his view, no treaty clauses had any value if a major power disregarded a treaty and wanted a test of strength. A treaty requiring that offenders meet with declarations of war by everybody else meant little; a world government regarding all wars as civil wars meant "not a damned thing".† For all the great questions of reform in the world order, this point is militarily and politically obvious; but by thinking legally rather than politically, the predominant western disarmament schools have given themselves the impossible and potentially dangerous task of speculating on how positive law could be enforced on great states. They have detached themselves from the real policies of governments into an unrealism which lacks even the merit of being utopian. Mr. Bernard G. Bechoefer, who was for many years a senior American disarmament negotiator, has written‡ that "Baruch's veto position is the extreme example of his isolation from the general currents of United States foreign policy". He was not isolated, however, from the powerful western legal tradition.

The obvious problem in giving political substance to international society is to find ways of involving strong individual units in an effective common life. These units are

* Ibid., p. 541.
† Ibid., p. 565.
‡ *Postwar Negotiations for Arms Control* (Washington, Brookings Institution, 1961), p. 60.

not going to be dominated by a heavily armed centre;* for even in the presence of far-reaching disarmament the decisive power would almost certainly remain in those national governments which could, if necessary, rely on the loyalty of their populations and organize their resources to resist. The term international security is therefore used here to mean something distinct from the familiar concept of collective security or from the idealist's hope of an international agency able to defend states against their enemies. The primacy of enforcement is so powerfully entrenched in people's minds that it is often regarded as the test of international security agencies. The League of Nations accepted this in full and judged itself by its success or failure at meeting military challenges. The United Nations excluded the great powers from its sphere of enforcement through the Security Council's rule of unanimity for permanent members: but for the rest the Security Council is still judged by its failure to keep the peace. Yet the U.N. on Rhodesia has been as impotent as the League on Abyssinia in spite of the unanimity with which the great powers have denied the legitimacy of the exercise of power by the Smith regime. If some substantial group of states wanted to undertake the military obligations (and submit themselves to the risks) of an enforcement agency, there is no reason why they should not do so. Alliances today have this character and could be reformed on a still wider or even universal basis. A grand alliance could be formed to make war on Mr. Smith, the South Africans or even the Chinese, as it was to make war on Herr Hitler. But this is not what is being discussed in this study. International security is approached here on a different basis. It is seen as the problem of reforming the power structure through common

* This conclusion, which is basic to the approach in this study, is fundamentally different from that of, for example, John Strachey, who states: "Somewhere, somehow, there will have to be a centre of power, wielded by somebody. And power must be read in this context as meaning nuclear power. Disarmament must play an indispensable part in the emergence of an organized world. But it must be the disarmament of everybody else before the armament of a single centre." *On the Prevention of War* (London, Macmillan, 1962), p. 284.

action so as to make the power system safer and possibly cheaper.

The corollary is that responsibility for confrontation and enforcement must rest on the states themselves or on groups of states made up to meet particular dangers. Many people would regard it as fundamentally retrograde to argue (*a*) that the only people able to deal with a major military challenge are those who see themselves as the rivals of the challenger; (*b*) that therefore national security systems must remain effective in relation to the threats their governments fear—threats either to themselves or to those to whom they feel committed; and (*c*) that if the major powers want to have a war there is nothing very much that any conceivable international security institution can do about it.* Nevertheless, these conclusions are unavoidable. So also is the conclusion that what governments believe to be the basis of their national security cannot be dismantled as part of the process of constructing international security. The hypothesis of the effort to build an international security system must be that states do not want a war; that if they get into one they will soon enough want to be extricated from it; and that the business of international society is to give permanent, effective and practical life to the common interest.

A further corollary is that the problems raised by the development of thermonuclear weapons cannot be resolved by nuclear disarmament or by the creation of a centrally controlled nuclear force. The subjective fact that certain important governments attach major (and justifiable) importance to their nuclear forces is unlikely to change. There are also certain unavoidable objective facts. If it is conceded that no central institutions can impose their will on a major power, such powers will have to take account of the potential as well as actual power of their rivals. Certain states have the knowledge and productive facilities to

---

* It might be added that the progress and outcome of such a war will not be influenced in any significant way by the support or hostility of a putative world public opinion as represented by some voting process for the representatives of states.

manufacture nuclear weapons and they will always have these. They will always, therefore, have these weapons or their potentiality whether or not the weapons are nominally abolished. If there are those who fear their use of such weapons, that use must be deterred by those threatened, since international institutions uttering nuclear threats, still less carrying them out, can be no part of any realistic international security order.

Many people would feel that to try to build an international security system which acknowledges the permanence of national nuclear forces is to abandon the great objective from the start. There is a widespread feeling that national nuclear forces (and the same applies to major conventional forces) are inconsistent with international security. We must hesitate, however, before any assumption that requires us to abandon what are thought to be the main elements in the present world security system, which is by common consent remarkably stable. A new structure which might increase the chances of war by eroding this stability (while incidentally depriving the world of the virtues of variety, choice, competition and sanctuary) is not automatically to be counted superior. It is perhaps also permissible to take into consideration the fact that, however desirable, the abolition of these forces is not negotiable with most or all of the greatest powers.

For an international structure to work effectively over a long period, it must clearly be capable of great flexibility. It will face the unpredictable and will have to respond successfully. Designing it is work for the Japanese rather than the European architect—a man who assumes that his building will have to withstand earthquakes. There will be the challenge of those new scientific developments which have implications for military power; and there may be threats deliberately mounted by the disaffected or the ambitious against the system itself. Any good military planner starts with the assumption that he has not thought of the challenge that will actually come: or that if he has he has probably ruled it out as unrealistic. The same will be true of a fabric of international security. It will need institutions capable of adaptation and improvisation.

If it is founded, however, on national security systems which are themselves stable it will have a fundamental strength. This strength can be maintained by reinforcing rather than liquidating this stability through the working of the international institutions themselves. With the development of the notion of stability in national security thinking, we may be approaching the situation in which the objectives of the major powers and many other powers can be aligned but it may be that this can only be achieved through the political working of international society.

This is not primarily a study of institutions or history or law: it is a study of power and how it might be organized. Armaments seldom if ever create the conditions in which a particular kind of political organization becomes inevitable; but the realities of power can impede a development which may on other grounds seem to be desirable. It is not the purpose of this study to say when the kind of conscious international security system it advocates might come into existence. It is a study of how certain elements of it could be constructed if fear of unintended war and fear of the spread of weapons of mass destruction should combine to persuade a decisive group of countries that they must find a safer way to organize force. It is an attempt to find the working principles and the first steps in the reform of power.

The approach is conservative and gradualist. However, the central problems have already taken shape and some of the lines along which they might be solved have already been indicated. With the United Nations, one obviously important piece of machinery has been constructed. Some elements in its design and experience may have rendered it permanently unfit for the security responsibilities for which it was primarily created: its voting pattern is divorced from the realities of power; there is a long history of resistance to specialized military staffs; and where security issues are concerned there has been a constant effort to use the U.N. to promote national interests rather than to work within the limits of the common interest. Nevertheless, the U.N. seems to have achieved one of the elements of strength in governments: the reputation for being (in spite of almost fatal weaknesses) an inevitable and even possibly permanent fact of life. If we create working security institutions in our time, they will no doubt be linked in some way to the U.N. security structure.

Other institutions are important for the lessons they teach. The North Atlantic Treaty Organization will be examined in this study as the outstanding example of an attempt by significant powers to create an international security system. While this only exists because of a common European-North American appreciation of a particular threat, its life has taught more general lessons. N.A.T.O. has established the classic cases of nuclear guarantees and, more generally, of the transmission of the security problems of certain countries into the security policy of others. Its sharing and planning arrangements, and its system of national forces committed to international commands, all indicate how a modern international security structure might evolve.

The economic institutions of the West—mainly the General Agreement on Tariffs and Trade, the International Monetary Fund, the Organization for Economic Cooperation and Development, the World Bank and its affiliates, and the Group of Ten—also teach important lessons. With them, as with any arrangements for international security, common interests must be found and then enforced through rules that enable those interests to be sustained against particular interests. There was no external stimulus, as with N.A.T.O.; yet they have handled issues which aroused political passions quite as great as those aroused by contemporary security problems among leading powers.

Since only a concert of powers can agree to disarm, all existing disarmament proposals can be said to be based on the assumption that a concert of the powers will have been achieved. Some seem to feel that a concert will come into existence in some better political atmosphere which is often associated with the disappearance of certain particularly bad or ignorant politicians; others foresee it as the product of fear, arising from growing evidence that the world order is breaking down into war and chaos. Disarmament thinking is also generally based on an assumption that a concert of the powers progressively arises as arms are reduced. The underlying premise is that armaments in rival states are the central cause of rivalry, that a concert gradually comes about as weapons and military threats are removed, and that this unity is completely achieved through stages of each which widens the area of agreement.* The reasoning behind this is unconvincing. A concert of the powers, willing or unwilling, is certainly needed to make disarmament agreements possible. But there is no reason to think that a concert follows disarmament and becomes more strongly established as a result of it. Indeed, if the traditional disarmament school is right and the early stages of disarmament relieve tension and reduce the risks, the concert should logically become harder to sustain.

The argument presented here works from different assumptions. While recognizing that real advances in international security depend on a readiness of the decisive powers to act in concert, it sees no need to wait for some better day before facing the problems of power. There is no reason to think that the international climate is certain to become better and some grounds for assuming that it is as good now as it can ever be expected to be. There is also an attempt to avoid reliance on optimistic assumptions about what happens when some level of agreement has been reached. But some of the consequences of the inevitable bad periods may be minimized. One hopeful element about power in our time is that international relations can remain good in one sphere while becoming bad in another. There is some evidence that (as in the eighteenth century) even a military conflict can be kept from influencing many aspects of relations between two countries. Co-operation remains possible in important spheres in a way that would have been regarded as unthinkable earlier in this century. Where there is a common interest, the powers can thus concert themselves without having to achieve a total agreement across all the

* In the familiar oratory, each stage "reduces tension", which is held to be the primary cause of armaments: this tension is almost always referred to, even when (as in the present Soviet-American confrontation) no tension is evident.

important areas of public policy. Total war has become meaningless: and therefore all conflict, at least between major powers, must in all circumstances be limited by the conscious restraint of the participants. The unity of policy—above all, the notion that the state of war is total—has broken down.

The importance of this for the concert of powers and so for arms control and disarmament agreements cannot be exaggerated. There can be a common effort on one range oi issues while rivalries continue on others. We are not obliged to wait for a formal alliance relationship to be established and extended to all subjects before we can begin to reform the world security system through concerted action. It is therefore desirable that common action for the common security should be removed from the arena in which it is forced to respond to the political climate of international life. Major new steps will always be political at the time they are taken and will obviously only be taken if the powers concerned welcome the political implications. But these can be consolidated and maintained in working arrangements even in the face of a drastic decline of international goodwill. An analogy is to be found in international trade agreements. At a time of bad relations governments on the two sides would not sign a dramatic new trade agreement, but there might nevertheless be steady progress in existing commercial relationships and even a rise in trade. It would all depend on whether what was essentially non-political and in the common interest had, for some reason, to be drawn up on to the political level. So long as it remains professional, the trade (like the postal services) can go on. Working international security arrangements are only possible if, in this sense, their continuous working is taken out of politics.

This is a matter of organization and attitude. Few countries consider membership in the United Nations to be a political issue responsive to their international policies. With isolated exceptions, the existence of the United Nations is taken for granted in the way that the League of Nations was not. We have advanced to the point where its existence has passed out of international politics. There is similarly no reason why broad and important advances in international security should not be made by the powers jointly in the presence of only a limited willingness to work in concert. This depends on achieving a professional relationship which is deliberately kept outside politics. A central argument advanced here is that the way forward is to create a central professional military organization to discover where the common security interest is and to administer it. Such an organization may eventually help to widen the area of concerted action but it should not depend for its creation on a pre-existing alliance relationship. A certain concert of the powers is needed, for example, to operate the International Civil Aviation Organization. Without such a concert, world aviation would be impossible. But this mutually valuable technical objective does not depend on dedication to perfect amity; nor has it required governments to concede ultimate control over their own air space. There was a common interest to be served; it required specialized technical skills; and the necessary organization was created in common to solve the common problems.

Once such an organization had come into existence in the security field and governments knew its working and understood its character, its responsibilities would expand to the extent that governments identified common security interests. In any one period that might be very much or very little, depending on the skill with which the institutions were managed and on the political climate in the world. No doubt there would be periods when the system would do well to survive and continue to discharge its most pressing obligations. But as in federal states, there would be a natural tendency for power to accumulate at the point at which problems could most easily be solved. All the evidence is that on the great security issues this would be at the centre.

The purpose of this study, then, is to see how an international security system might be created over a period of time without dismantling the present one, as this is understood by governments, and without any particular change in the Soviet-American political climate. It rests on the thesis that there is no irreconcilable element in the present system

—an assumption which in turn depends on the belief that there is no group of powers which is ready to challenge the *status quo* by war. China, Western Europe, Japan and possibly others may eventually seek ways of altering the international system, such as it is. But the evidence at present is that the *status quo* is difficult to challenge except by successful political penetration of other countries in which the large-scale use of force plays only a small part. In the presence of nuclear weapons, the kind of challenge that Japan and Germany made to the *status quo* of the 1930s is probably excluded. Lesser military options are still taken up from time to time by both major and minor powers. A world working on the sort of rules now being applied can be reasonably safe or very dangerous depending on what choices governments make in the use of force. Disarmament and arms control agreements, whether formal or tacit, are about what governments can do in concert to ameliorate this situation. Though this study is made on the assumption that there are strong secular forces pushing the major powers into concert over important areas of security policy whether they like it or not, it is not concerned with trying to prove that they will give way to these forces. It is intended to suggest a possible approach to the organization of power in the event that the *status quo* is predominant and the major powers recognize that they must work together.

Those who are interested enough to follow the argument may .wish to know its main origins. The approach was developed in the course of three different pieces of research. The first concerned nuclear proliferation, on which I reached two main conclusions: that abstention from nuclear weapons on the part of the five or six powers which can make them now (and a growing number in the future) will depend on their sense of participation in the working of a security system led by the great powers; and that the spread of plutonium and uranium enrichment plants to many non-industrial countries as a by-product of nuclear power programmes can only be avoided by the development of a world atomic energy system based on international ownership of fissile materials. The second was a study of the problem of alliances (specifically, the North Atlantic alliance) in the light of modern strategic doctrine. This suggested that the inner life of N.A.T.O. provides the most instructive precedents for how a working alliance of most or all of the powers in the world might work—far more instructive, for example, than the familiar analogy of national governments. The third was an attempt to apply the first stages of the Soviet and American general disarmament plans to the N.A.T.O. and Warsaw Pact forces in Europe. This study convinced me that these plans were divorced from real security thought and rested on the false premise that world security problems would be simplified as national weapons were destroyed and armed forces reduced. The western plan also rested on an image of a world government that seemed impossible to achieve and that would be unlikely, in any case, to have the characteristics which the stable political societies of the authors of these plans (generally the United States and Britain) associate with government.

It was clear that those plans were never intended to be taken seriously. Few if any of their authors were under any illusions. What this revealed, however, was that with all the great devotion and energy which governments are putting into maintaining the security order almost no thought or effort is going into speculation about how it might realistically be reformed.

This study is an attempt to suggest ways in which a predominant group of governments might reform the power they control so as to meet the realities of the world as it appears to be evolving.

2

THE NEED FOR REFORM

WITH all its dangers, the world today appears very much more secure than anyone believed possible when the conflict between the Soviet Union and the West became serious in the late 1940s. Unfortunately, it is very difficult to know just how secure it is. The warning that it is on the brink of self-destruction has been repeated constantly over the years by the advocates of disarmament, and especially of nuclear disarmament; orthodoxy has relied on what it hoped would prove to be a balance of terror. On the whole, it must be said that the bold predictions of those who said there would and could be no general war have been more successfully borne out by events since 1950 than the fears of their critics. All major governments have in practice accepted the assumptions of the advocates of deterrence. They have armed themselves heavily, especially with weapons of mass destruction, while arguing that this could and should lead to a more stable world with a small chance of central war. They have not yet been proved wrong. The accidental use of nuclear weapons has been confined to fiction; even so serious a miscalculation as the Russian missile initiative in Cuba was put right without conflict; and most people would agree that the balance of terror, so-called, has moderated the behaviour of the major powers in every military situation which has developed since the Second World War.

As a result, it seems true to say that most sovereign states believe that in the present situation they have a substantial measure of external security. There are important exceptions to this: a number of countries (such as Israel, Jordan, Syria, the U.A.R., India, North and South Vietnam, Malaysia, Pakistan, Zambia and Cuba) fear hostile and powerful neighbours; others fear subversion or revolution. As the

Egyptians have shown in the Yemen, the Israelis in Sinai and the Chinese on the Indian border, some military adventuring remains possible. But, even in these areas, so distant from the primary concerns of the great powers, there are strong inhibitions to going too far. If the major powers are drawn in, the campaign could become disastrous and the aggressor could inflict on himself and everyone else the terrible retribution of a breakdown in the world order. Since 1950, we have had five armed conflicts which related directly to the East–West confrontation: the Korean War, the Russian occupations of Hungary and Czechoslovakia, the American quarantine of Cuba, and the American intervention in Vietnam. In Korea and Cuba, these seem to have stemmed directly from miscalculations or from a decision that the precise commitment of the other side was sufficiently unclear to be worth challenging. Once the challenge was accepted, the conflict was carefully limited. In Hungary and Czechoslovakia, there was no miscalculation and the campaign proceeded to a quick and decisive conclusion. In Vietnam, the Americans correctly calculated that other great powers would not intervene but miscalculated the effect of their own power.

There have also been four continuing states of war or near war over post-colonial situations in which the British did not achieve general agreement before granting independence and two in which the independence arrangements of the British and Belgians were challenged. These are the Israel–Arab conflict, the India–Pakistan conflict, the Indonesia–Malaysia conflict, the strained relations of Greece and Turkey over Cyprus, and the civil wars in the Congo and Nigeria. The Americans and Russians made an effort to stay out of all these; and in each case the United Nations was brought in at an early stage. Although most of these situations have not been successfully resolved, working arrangements have been achieved from time to time; and it has become generally accepted that the world order was not in danger. This says a great deal for the basic stability which the world in its present form has achieved.

The record of the thermonuclear age is therefore distinctly

encouraging. The balance of terror has worked and is likely in most circumstances to go on working. If this is true (and most governments believe it is) no one concerned for world security and the survival of nations can possibly dismiss it. All proposals for disarmament and arms control must be measured against it. Those which dismantle the present security system will have to show that they will replace it with something safer.

Equally, however, the existing system presents real dangers actual and potential. Proposals for change must be tested not only for their ability to preserve the strengths of the present order but also for their value in removing or diminishing the weaknesses. Among others, six main problems are of obvious concern:

1. The possibility that technology will at some point make disarming nuclear strikes a real or apparent possibility or will make this avoidable only by adopting dangerous tactics.

2. The spread of nuclear weapons to the control of many governments and possibly beyond governments.

3. The possibility of accidental or unauthorized use of nuclear weapons or civil war in a nuclear power.

4. The development and spread of new techniques of mass destruction.

5. The possibility of a serious miscalculation leading to large-scale hostilities between major powers.

6. The involvement of the major powers in a local conflict over which they lose control through their own actions or those of their allies.

Each of these will be looked at in turn with the aim (in subsequent chapters) of seeing what changes in the organization of power might minimize these risks.

I   *The disarming nuclear strike*

The invention and development of nuclear weapons have created a uniquely difficult range of problems. Their immense destructiveness has given the main nuclear powers the ability to destroy a large part of the society of enemy

29

countries. The psychological effect of this has been to impart security to the possessors of these forces far more than insecurity to those who are threatened. In the case of the United States (and her main allies), this has gone so far as to make what the U.S. Defense Department calls an assured destruction capability the first priority of defence policy. Successive American administrations have been equally ready to concede that the Soviet Union possesses— and, in effect, should possess—an equivalent capacity for destruction in the United States. The notion of the balance of terror has become established under a name which sounds much more agreeable: a stable confrontation. The doctrine of stability has been stated and re-stated in American defence doctrine for many years. One example, from Mr. Robert McNamara (Secretary of Defense, 1961–67), will suffice:*

"It is generally agreed that a vital first objective, to be met in full by our strategic nuclear forces, is the capability for Assured Destruction. Such a capability would, with a high degree of confidence, ensure that we could deter under all foreseeable conditions a calculated, deliberate nuclear attack upon the United States. What kinds and amounts of destruction we would have to be able to inflict in order to provide this assurance cannot be answered precisely. But it seems reasonable to assume that the destruction of, say, one-quarter to one-third of its population and about two-thirds of its industrial capacity would mean the elimination of the aggressor as a major power for many years. Such a level of destruction would certainly represent intolerable punishment to any industrialized nation and thus should serve as an effective deterrent."

The Soviet Union has never publicly abandoned the belief that the central objective in war, and so the heart of Soviet defence policy, is to defeat the fighting forces of the enemy. Nevertheless, as in the West, great debates have taken place between the conventional soldiers and the

* Statement before the House Armed Services Committee on the 1966–70 Defense Program and 1966 Defense Budget, 18 February 1965, official report, p. 39.

advocates of nuclear deterrence. A dual position has on the whole been maintained; and a good public statement of it is to be found in Marshal Sokolovsky:*

"The question arises of what constitutes the main strategic goal of the war: the defeat of the enemy's armed forces (as in the past) or the annihilation, destruction and devastation in the enemy's rear for the purpose of disorganizing it? Soviet strategic theory gives the following answer: both these goals should be achieved simultaneously. The annihilation of the enemy's armed forces, the destruction of objectives in the rear and disorganization of the rear will be a single continuous process of war."

The feeling of nuclear power is also expressed in this passage:†

"The build-up of nuclear stocks and the widespread introduction of these weapons in all branches of the armed forces enable the strategic command to use them simultaneously to inflict massive losses on the armed forces of the aggressor, to destroy his material and technical base for waging war, and to disrupt his government and military administration."

Obviously the United States and the Soviet Union would have an effective defence policy in the absence of thermonuclear weapons. Nevertheless they have both become heavily dependent in their own minds on their assured capacity for destruction. They know, or think they know, that no matter what happens they will be able to wreak terrible destruction on anyone who strikes heavily at their central interests. They believe that such an attack therefore becomes an act so lacking in sanity as to make it exceedingly unlikely. No element in the international order is more important than this belief. In the American case, in particular, it can be said that no foreseeable American government will allow its assured destruction capability (in the worst imaginable case) to be undermined. One can argue about what the assumptions of the worst case should be and also

* *Military Strategy, Soviet Doctrine and Concepts,* ed. Marshal V. D. Sokolovsky (London, Pall Mall; New York, Praeger, 1963), p. 495.

† Ibid., p. 187.

about just how many people one has to be able to kill to have an effective deterrent. But these are arguments about the definition of the thing, not the thing itself.

From the earliest days of nuclear weapons there has been a tendency for these weapons to remove what they themselves have conferred. As they have become more powerful and more accurate, they have increasingly threatened to deprive opponents of any capacity for assured destruction they might have. The American and British air forces, whose bomber arms were developed on secure bases during the Second World War, were reluctant for a long time to accept that the nuclear weapons which were making them so powerful were also making them vulnerable. They resisted the growing pressure in the middle-1950s for a drastic approach to the problem of survival in the face of a surprise attack. It was argued that the variety of American and British bases would make it impossible for a coordinated attack to be launched.

The warnings came most authoritatively and most systematically from the Rand Corporation, where a fundamental study of air bases had produced disturbing conclusions.* By the late 1950s, as the Soviet force became equipped with thermonuclear weapons and Soviet rocketry had made great advances, the case had become generally accepted in Washington. No doubt the Soviet debate followed similar lines: though the earlier emergence of strategic nuclear forces in the West and their larger numbers must have given those who warned of Soviet vulnerability a persuasive case at an earlier date.

Since that time, solutions to this difficulty have been sought and found in many directions and have absorbed a large amount of technological effort. They have become the central element in strategic nuclear arms development: and it is therefore no exaggeration to say that they are the single most important concern in American and Soviet security policy. As this issue lies at the heart of international

---

* The main conclusions of this study by its principal author were first published in Albert Wohlstetter, "The Delicate Balance of Terror", *Foreign Affairs*, vol. 37, January, 1959.

security and as it is by no means resolved, it must be looked at in some detail.

Over a 15-year period, the Americans have spent enormous sums of money on spreading their bombers over many bases, maintaining an airborne alert, maintaining a large force at 15-minute readiness on the ground, building concrete silos for ballistic missiles, and developing missile-firing nuclear-powered submarines. Other solutions—mounting Minuteman land-based ballistic missiles on trains, Polaris missiles in cruisers, and the Skybolt airborne ballistic missile development—have been tried and dropped. The programme of ballistic missile defences for the 1970s has been specifically directed to the defence of the land-based bomber and missile forces in the event that a direct Russian threat to their survival should emerge.

Although the Soviet Union has been the subject of a much more serious challenge to its strategic nuclear forces, it has responded less rapidly with invulnerable weapons. In the 1950s the whole effort was towards bigger offensive weapons and better defensive weapons. Mr. McNamara was able to say in 1963:* "Today we know that the great majority of the Soviet strategic force, both their bombers and their missiles, are in soft configurations." This remained largely true for the next five years, though major efforts were made in anti-missile defences.

The British nuclear planners became concerned by the problem of vulnerability soon after their first atomic bombers entered service in 1955. As the country possessed an unusually large number of airfields, an extensive dispersion programme was developed: and the pilots perfected take-offs from ground alerts (which were constantly maintained) in two minutes—the minimum period of expected radar warning of missile attack. The Royal Air Force was so confident about this technique for avoiding destruction on the ground from Soviet missiles at little more than 1000 miles range that it decided to go through the 1970s on this basis, equipping its medium bombers with the American

* Hearings on Military Posture, House Armed Services Committee, 1963, p. 332.

Skybolt as a means of increasing their penetration capability but not of decreasing their vulnerability. This plan had to be abandoned when the Skybolt was cancelled; and the British adopted the Polaris missile, mounting it in submarines of a type similar to those designed by the United States Navy.

The French are following the American solutions even more exactly: bombers, land-based ballistic missiles and submarine-based weapons. It is not clear yet how the Chinese propose to handle the very considerable problem of vulnerability they will face, particularly if they must take into account both Soviet and American capabilities.

These solutions to the problem of vulnerability divide themselves into two broad categories: fixed systems and mobile systems. In the 1960s the general position was that fixed systems appeared to be cheaper while mobile ones were less vulnerable. In the best documented case (the American one), large numbers of fixed missiles were acquired because this appeared to confer the security of numbers: it was too big a problem to attack them all. (They were also more accurate and had a larger payload.) But the real hopes of a secure, invulnerable force were placed in mobile systems, and particularly missile-firing submarines. This situation may now change, as the estimates of each period have tended to change in the past. If the effort to construct ballistic missile defences succeeds to any extent, the beneficiaries will be land-based ballistic missiles. Counting the cost of their defences, what was once the cheap option will then have become the most expensive form of strategic nuclear force.

The President of the United States took the position in 1970 that the fixed based nuclear weapon could no longer be made secure by hardening. Increases in accuracy and explosive power had reached the point (on U.S. estimates) where any point is vulnerable to attack, however strongly emplaced. Even if this is not true, there can be no doubt that it will be in future. The invention of nuclear weapons is irreversible and so is the invention of missiles with accuracies which must steadily increase. The critical question then becomes one of numbers; and this is obviously a function of the number of weapons that must be fired to destroy each missile position. If the weapons to be destroyed are spread out individually over a large area, the number of independent explosives required to destroy them with a high degree of certainty will inevitably exceed the number of weapons to be defended. But if the weapons are concentrated (either because they have multiple warheads or are on bases with several rockets) the number required to destroy them could be substantially less than one for one. A demonstration of this was provided by the original deployment of American bombers on airfields with 90 or more aircraft. Such a force could have been wiped out by an enemy force with very much smaller numbers.

The development of fixed land-based weapons has not unfortunately been towards the wide dispersal which would have made each side incapable of a disarming strike. For a variety of reasons, it has been uneconomical to spread a weapon such as the Minuteman missile out across wide areas; and since multiple warheads create new weapons but no new targets, their development and deployment on both sides of a rocket confrontation will inevitably result in a sharp increase in the ratio of attacking weapons to targets. Improvements in accuracy and in the numbers and explosive power of the multiple warheads must work steadily to worsen this situation and it is reasonable to assume that a force with inferior numbers will once again be capable of destroying a large force in a sudden attack.

Another way to preserve the effectiveness of fixed land-based missiles is to design and build active defences against enemy attack. The United States has turned its ballistic missile defence (or A.B.M.) efforts to the direct defence of the Minuteman sites. Although strongly criticized by those concerned about stability, this responds as well as any other likely solution to the need to maintain an assured destruction capability in Soviet hands. A.B.M. defence of cities (the original Johnson-McNamara plan) would obviously lead to substantial increases in a Soviet force designed to destroy American cities. As the effectiveness of the A.B.M. system

35

must be in doubt to everyone, including its owner, the need to overwhelm in the worst case by large numbers of decoys and missiles must substantially increase the force on the other side. Since the increase will be made on pessimistic assumptions, the resulting force must appear excessive to the rival whose pessimistic assumptions will be very different. It will be assumed that the new forces are very menacing or at any rate that they confer formidable new counterforce capabilities. In the Soviet–American confrontation, this insecurity cycle may already have begun. The Soviet Union may well have constructed its new missile forces in anticipation of the original Sentinel programme for a ballistic missile defence of some American cities.

President Nixon's plan for a ballistic missile defence specifically tied to the Minuteman sites bears all the marks of an effort to achieve common interests in the face of these developments in the U.S.S.R. A Soviet Union which cherished no disarming ambitions towards the United States —one, that is, which was prepared to concede the Americans their assured destruction capability—should have no desire to destroy American rockets on the ground.* President Nixon attempted to lay the foundations for a bargain by laying down a gradual programme for his own defences which was specifically linked to the development of the Soviet offensive force.

The construction of this American argument in international rather than national security language is evidence of the extent to which the need for common action has been accepted intellectually at the government level in the United States. While it must be recognized that the situation is not quite so pure as President Nixon would make out, it is certainly one that the Americans hope will be the subject of effective negotiations. The qualifications that must be made are that the Minuteman force has a large element of counterforce in it; that the Safeguard system is not confined to the Minuteman sites, as shown by the President's claim

---

* This argument is inevitably modified if it is argued that part or all of the Minuteman force is designed to destroy the Soviet armed forces, and particularly the rocket force.

that "this system will provide a defence of the Continental United States against an accidental attack and will provide substantial protection against the kind of attack which the Chinese Communists may be capable of launching throughout the 1970s"; and that with the American capacity for mass production it is inevitable that the Soviet authorities will assume that something which can provide a good defence of a Minuteman site can quickly and effectively be produced and deployed for the protection of cities.

One of the issues raised by the vulnerability problem is how urgently a force must be fired to avoid destruction. Planners seeking to build a force which need not fear surprise attack can aim for three different objectives:

1. A force which cannot be reliably destroyed in a sudden surprise attack because it can be fired on warning.

2. A force which can accept attack and can also be held for the period required for a high-level political decision to fire.

3. A force which cannot in any circumstances be destroyed and which can remain a force in being during major hostilities.

Obviously, one way of avoiding the risk of destruction on the ground is to hold the weapons at a high state of readiness and then fire them on radar information of attack. This would undoubtedly provide a high assurance that a good proportion would escape destruction by the attacking missiles. It would constitute, however, a serious continuing danger. To fire in these circumstances means firing with no effective intervention of responsible political judgement. Any human decision there might be would be at the level of military officers, no doubt at times of junior rank. Any heavy nuclear force which cannot be held back until the full realities of what has happened—and that means with all the thought which a great government can bring to bear— before being launched is self-evidently badly designed. Official American opinion at all levels has held this view for many years. The need "to ride out any attack" (a phrase used in 1957 by the Commander of the Strategic Air Command) and then retaliate was fully accepted in the middle

1950s and has informed all thought and planning ever since. It is difficult to find public statements in the Soviet Union, Britain or France to show that this has been recognized by these three governments. Weakness and vulnerability discourage assurances to potential enemies; and it is to be hoped that this rather than a failure to understand the risks is the reason for the lack of public commitment to deliberation in the face of an attack. It may be that there is an important difference between declaratory policy and real policy in these three countries. But there are dangers in this. Declaratory policy may or may not be believed by possible enemies: it is almost certain to be believed by the ordinary people manning one's own services. Politicians up to the highest levels of authority can belong to the simple rather than the sophisticated school of contemporary strategic thought.*

Some degree of vulnerability to enemy strike also raises important questions about the kind of war strategy nuclear powers will adopt. Although all nuclear powers seek a capacity for massive retaliation and some try to exploit the deterrent effect of threatening to use it in a wide variety of situations, it is clear that there is a wide margin between the declaratory and the real. Those who favour unambiguous threats of maximum destruction are confident that these will not be put to the test. They argue, in effect, that a sufficiently powerful deterrent makes unnecessary a war plan designed to minimize damage. The evidence is now generally available, however, that all the governments that have given thought to the question are anxious to be in a position to respond to any war situation controllably and with the intention of limiting damage. If this is accepted, it creates a new and much more severe test for an adequate nuclear force. It must not only be able to survive a massive surprise attack but it must also be able to survive through partial nuclear conflict in which limited strikes of many kinds are

* The academic study of strategic problems suffers from the links between scholars and the most intelligent elements in the government service. It is often implicitly assumed that since these people comprehend the problems they also possess the power.

launched. A deterrent safe from destruction becomes not just a peacetime objective but also a wartime need. The nuclear power in search of security thus requires not just an assured destruction capability, but one which can be retained as a force in being in any circumstances which might be created by an enemy.

It is in this context that the fixed missile force with ballistic missile defences must be studied: and to those without access to classified information (and probably also for those with it) no firm estimate is possible. The effectiveness of ballistic missile defences will grow continuously over the years, as will the techniques for penetrating them. This balance is not only unforeseeable but will probably not be known at any given point in time by the principal actors. Too many elements in it will be untested and (in the enemy case) unobserved. It would seem likely, however, that ballistic missile defences will themselves be too vulnerable—at a minimum through the vulnerability of their radars—for a fixed land-based force dependent on them to be expected to remain safe for a substantial period of war. A disturbing amount of thought and debate in the United States about the question of ballistic missile defence for the land-based retaliatory force has slipped back into the assumption that a nuclear force is designed to be fired massively and early; and that as long as this can be counted on, the assured destruction capability exists.* Because of the persistence of these unattractive strategies in declaratory policy, the debate about future weapons tends to be conducted on these less

* A remarkable example of this is to be found in *ABM: An Evaluation of the Decision to Deploy an Antiballistic Missile System*, under the name of Dr. Jerome B. Wiesner (New York, Signet, 1969), p. 74. In developing his case against the U.S. A.B.M. programme, he states: "If one is truly worried about a full-scale SS–9 attack, it is possible to launch the Minuteman and Titan missiles after unequivocal warning of a large attack is received but before the attacking missiles have hit." He feels that the U.S. would "almost certainly have a clear warning at least 30 minutes in advance should the Soviets launch a massive first strike". Dr. Wiesner was President Kennedy's science adviser and is looked to for leadership by many Americans who would like to see a radical approach to the problems of power.

demanding assumptions. Clearly, however, anything other than the force in being able to survive in any circumstances is dangerous.

In addition to the fixed base on land, there is the possibility of fixed bases on the sea-bed, a possibility which has received some attention in recent years. It is difficult to see what advantage it offers. Any solution which produced unmanned strategic systems in an international environment would suffer from major defects; lack of proper control over firing orders; poor communications; inadequate servicing and maintenance; accessibility to other powers. Such weapons would be both accident-prone and liable to be stolen. The controllable use of the sea-bed for weapons might emerge if deep undersea caves were dug into the rock and sealed with pressurized doors. These could no doubt ultimately be made into habitable military bases. One function of such establishments would be to free missile-firing submarines from the need to go into dockyards in time of emergency, and these bases might ultimately be used for replenishing their weapons. Obviously such undertakings are a long way off; and it may be doubted whether they could easily be constructed secretly in international waters, though this might be possible in inland seas like Hudson Bay. In the absence of secrecy, such bases would be exceptionably vulnerable and therefore presumably valueless. It is difficult to foresee any effective form of defence for them.

For fixed bases as a whole, therefore, the problem of maintaining a force in being against any possible opposition is very severe. Over the years, there is no real hope that it can be done except through restraint by opponents. The balance of effort in providing defences and improving offensive penetration will no doubt provide periods when one force (or both) is in a position to survive any attack; but even in such periods governments may not be certain that this would be the case if put to the test of war.

Much effort has gone into mobile systems in all the main nuclear powers. The United States has studied the possibilities seriously on land and sea and also in the air and in space.

The Soviet Union has also experimented at least with land and sea and almost certainly with space. While the two powers have reached the same conclusion at sea—the nuclear-powered missile-firing submarine with 16 missiles in each—they have experimented with differing solutions on land. The main American programme was for a train-mounted missile while the Soviet Union has put its efforts into road mobility in trucks. No doubt this difference of approach reflects the difficulties which the American authorities contemplated in using public roads to transport major missile systems. A road mobile system was, however, favoured by the European Allied Command of N.A.T.O. in the late 1950s. On political grounds, this was subsequently rejected in favour of concentration on sea-based systems, though these too were not in the end carried through.

Mobility on either road or rail implies weapons which are exposed on the surface. Satellite photography has undoubtedly made it possible to track the movement of weapons in this way fairly continuously. It is possible that at considerable expense and effort a sufficient number of false targets could be created to provide identification problems, at least for a road mobile system. But with the range of destruction and the precision of modern weapons, the land mobile system clearly has grave disadvantages. The Soviet Union has recognized this by going over increasingly to hardened missiles—that is to say, to fixed concrete silos.

Mobility on the surface of the sea is open to the same objections, reinforced by the much greater ease with which satellites can track surface ships. The background of water makes a target which is exceptionally difficult to confuse. In addition, tracking by aircraft, ship and submarine is unrestricted because of the right of navigation in and over the high seas. One of the first acts of the Kennedy Administration when it took power in the United States in 1961 was to scrap the plan to put Polaris missiles into a cruiser. No doubt nothing more would have been heard of the surface ship missile base had it not been for the extensive argumentation which was advanced in connection with the plan for a N.A.T.O. multilateral force of 25 merchant-type ships carrying eight Polaris missiles each. The military doctrines advanced in Washington when the formation of this force was U.S. policy lacked the professionalism that has become an accepted part of the American approach to these matters.

It may be that the Americans favoured the force on political grounds while mistrusting it enough to want it to remain ineffective. There may, indeed, have been a school of opinion in Washington which considered it an advantage that in some unforeseen future (especially if the United States withdrew from the force in favour of united European ownership and command) the ships would be easy to destroy in a crisis. In playing at the design of a Frankenstein monster, weapons system analysts could well be expected to recommend a destruction mechanism.

No hint of ballistic missiles mounted in flying machines has emerged from the Soviet Union: and the American project for such a weapon, Skybolt, was cancelled in 1962 after attracting strong interest from both the United States Air Force and the Royal Air Force. Nevertheless, it would be a mistake to assume that this solution to the problem of organizing a heavy nuclear force in being has been discredited. Skybolt looked as if it would be an expensive programme because it was tied to the American B-52H and British Vulcan 2 bombers, both of which had been designed as high-performance penetration bombers and were costly to maintain in the air for long patrols. A long endurance dromedary would show more acceptable costs. The advantages of this system may well lead at some future date to further experimentation with it. As with land mobile weapons, it does not need to operate in an international medium where extensive means of tracking (and also of non-nuclear attack) are open to rivals and enemies. It also shares with land-based systems the advantage of reliable and efficient communications and effective physical control in the hands of the government which owns the weapons. While satellite tracking may not be avoided indefinitely, the difficulty of destroying a fleet of aircraft moving through extensive air space is obviously very great. Vertical take-off and landing could also liberate such a fleet from a limited number of air bases. The Skybolt showed that there are real problems to be solved in producing the airborne ballistic missile and in achieving the precision necessary to effective launching. Nevertheless, in the search for a force in being which can survive the tremendous advances in numbers and accuracy which are now going on, the airborne ballistic missile may prove to be one of the few hopeful cards left to play.

Weapons in orbit might be regarded as either a fixed or a mobile base. Clearly they move very rapidly (in relation to the earth); but equally they remain in a predictable orbit and are therefore in a real sense fixed. However one regards them, they clearly provide no solution to the problem of creating a force in being. They are in a position where they are easily detectable; they will normally pass over enemy territory from time to time where they can easily be destroyed; they are liable to be approached and possibly damaged, destroyed, examined or stolen by rival orbiting vehicles; and if unmanned they will be very expensive to maintain and keep efficient. It is not surprising that the United States, the Soviet Union and the United Kingdom so easily negotiated and signed the first paragraph of Article 4 of the Treaty on Principles Governing the Activities of States in the Exploration and Use of Outer Space, including the Moon and Other Celestial Bodies, which reads:*

States Parties to the Treaty undertake not to place in orbit around the earth any objects carrying nuclear weapons or any other kinds of weapons of mass destruction, install such weapons on celestial bodies, or station such weapons in outer space in any other manner.

Judged in terms of governmental decision and finance, there can be no doubt that the most important—indeed, the only important—form of mobile heavy nuclear force to be developed up to the present is the missile-firing submarine. The United States has built 41 of these, the Soviet Union is building at the rate of about 4 a year, the United Kingdom has built four and France is building a similar number. The

* This Treaty was signed on 27 January 1967. Its text is published as Cmd. 7015, H.M.S.O., London.

advantages of this form of missile base are well known: it has two-thirds of the earth's surface in which to move; it can vary its depths; it can manoeuvre very rapidly and move faster than its surface pursuers; it can find concealment behind layers of water, under the Arctic ice, or in the exploitation of the immense variety of the ocean floor. These advantages have led governments which were concerned at the growing capacity of their rivals to destroy their bombers and fixed-based missiles on the ground to invest heavily in these submarines. The cost has been substantial. Official American figures released in 1962 (when the major decisions were being made to build the 41-boat Polaris fleet) gave the cost of procurement, training and deployment for five years of five nuclear submarines with 80 Polaris as $1,000,000,000. For this same price, the U.S. could acquire 250 Minutemen in hard silos and maintain them for five years. Unit costs for each Polaris missile were therefore three times as great as those for Minuteman; and this had to be increased by a factor of perhaps a third because of the long periods which submarines must inevitably spend in the dockyard. The United States was thus spending heavily on the undetectable mobility of the Polaris-firing submarine.* This is the measure of the vulnerability problem as the least vulnerable power saw it in the early 1960s.

While the missile-firing submarine now stands as the classic solution to the vulnerability problem, it is by no means secure. Fears for the viability of these submarines as a reliable force in being have grown slowly but steadily; and there have always been certain elements of real concern. These might be summarized as follows:

1. Submarines must in large measure live in an international medium where an enemy is free to shadow or track them.

---

* Since the Minuteman remained invulnerable through the early years of operation of this fleet, because the Soviet Union did not produce enough delivery systems to mount a threat to them, it might be said that the Polaris expenditure was in retrospect unnecessary in that phase. The effort was part of the familiar process of insuring against a worst case which does not emerge.

2. If a submarine disappears, it is difficult to know whether the cause was accidental or due to some warlike act; and even if there is a strong suspicion that it was attacked, it is difficult to identify either the means employed or the power responsible.

3. This suggests that a general attack against an enemy's missile-firing submarine fleet need not be perfectly co-ordinated and simultaneous.

4. Submarines are subject to several forms of non-nuclear attack and can be destroyed without recourse to nuclear weapons.

5. General techniques of ocean surveillance through the propagation of sound, acoustic devices on the ocean bed, alterations in the earth's magnetic field and other methods are attracting large resources and showing steady improvement. The range at which a given volume of sound can be heard has gone up spectacularly. The listening and tracking qualities of the nuclear submarine itself are steadily improving; and the homing torpedo (an unmanned submarine used as an anti-submarine guided weapon) can be expected to increase its range, speed and performance as the years go on.

6. The growth of thermonuclear weapons of immense explosive power raises the possibility of a vast co-ordinated attack on large areas of ocean with the intention of raising intolerable pressures. This awesome tactic would no doubt make most sense for a country like the Soviet Union, which had least to fear from tidal waves.

7. Missile-firing submarines have a serious problem of communication. Unless a dangerous amount of initiative is given to their commanders, they are vulnerable to attacks on the high-powered radio transmitters which are necessary to give them orders while submerged.

8. Submarine-based missiles are restricted in both space and weight and the earlier generation of Polaris missiles proved to be particularly sensitive to ballistic missile defences. The attempt to overcome this problem by developing the multiple warhead Poseidon led to a loss of range (restricting the areas of water available for submarines

capable of operations) and substantial sacrifices in explosive power.

9. Several powers already have missile-firing submarines at sea and this number will increase. This must create difficulties of identification in the event that one or more of the missiles is fired.

10. Because of the very wide range of operational uncertainties, a power will have to act on the assumption that the other side has solved the problem of targeting and destroying its missile-firing submarines long before this has in practice been achieved. Thus the assurance of invulnerability (the source of security) must disappear some time before a submarine force has in fact become vulnerable.

These are the difficulties of the system which is by common consent the least vulnerable. As these difficulties increase, there is little that can be done for the submarine, apart from the slow improvement in silencing techniques and the development of new materials allowing them to operate at greater depths and to be able to fire from greater ranges. The simple physical vastness of the oceans remains, of course, especially if the navies operating these submarines could learn to serve their own tradition of the force in being: at present they are confining themselves to narrow seas because of a doctrine of massive and instant retaliation which their governments would abandon in a real war situation and which could deny their country the decisive element in negotiating an end to hostilities.

All in all, it is difficult to avoid the conclusion that maintaining an assured destruction capability will test the resources of major powers if they are up against rivals determined to limit their capacity to do damage. The nuclear force in being, able to survive anything that can be done to it, exists now. Because the anti-submarine forces and the missile forces capable of wiping out hundreds of hardened land-based weapons do not exist, the United States, the Soviet Union and Britain all possess substantial second-strike forces. Each can absorb the worst the others can offer and still retain a capacity to do immense damage.

In this situation, the product of anxious fears about

vulnerability in the 1950s and the resulting weapons produced in the 1960s, the advantage of striking first in major war is at a minimum. In a situation in which all major nuclear forces were either safe from attack or could only be destroyed by expending the attacker's forces, the advantage of striking first would disappear. Developments since the late 1950s have given western governments the conviction that whatever might be the strategic intentions of the Soviet Union, no realistic aggressive options are open to it if these might involve major nuclear war. The Soviets probably now have the technical basis for a similar conviction about the United States. These material facts must and do mean more to governments than a score of non-aggression pacts, mutual security treaties, or pledges of coexistence. To know that by any reckoning the other side cannot profit from a surprise attack, and to know that he realizes this, is to have the greatest assurance any government can hope to have that it will not be attacked. This lifts urgency from the mechanism of response to an attack (or what might seem to be an attack). The immense assurance of the United States in the middle-1960s accounts for its public abandonment of the so-called massive retaliation doctrine and its gradual persuasion of the European N.A.T.O. allies that N.A.T.O. too should adopt a doctrine of flexible response. It is this kind of assurance that will remove any temptation to respond militarily to evidence through intelligence or other means that an enemy might be planning a surprise attack.

All the tendencies suggested above indicate, however, that left to the traditional rivalry and the accidents of innovation the mutual second-strike position cannot be relied on as permanent. Vast new intelligence-gathering methods, steadily improving accuracy and multiplying warheads are eroding the security of those who are inventing them. A technological age which has favoured survival and concealment—with all their political benefits—has left technological innovation with a benign reputation among those concerned with security. It will be surprising if the coming decade or two show that this reputation is justified.

II *The spread of nuclear weapons*

The problems raised by the prospect of a spread of nuclear weapons around the world are basic to the international order of the future. This has been recognized by the main powers since the evidence emerged at Alamogordo, New Mexico, in July 1945, that an explosive of unprecedented power had been made possible by the production of the new and artificial element, plutonium. The fact that the same thing could be done by the isolation of Uranium 235 from the uranium found in nature* was demonstrated shortly afterwards in the raid on Hiroshima. Although these processes had cost large amounts of money and had taken more than three years of intensive effort, it seemed obvious to those who understood what had happened that they raised profoundly difficult political problems. The attempt to find solutions to these problems began with the Baruch Plan and has continued with a wide variety of international proposals, culminating in the partial nuclear test ban of 1963 and the Non-Proliferation Treaty of 1968. It has also led to a complex international atomic energy system in which those supplying plant and materials have insisted on safeguards against the diversion of these to weapons.

Admirable as these efforts have been, they will not solve the problem of proliferation. Neither the Non-Proliferation Treaty (assuming it is signed by the decisive countries) nor the safeguards system will seriously inhibit a country which is in a position to build nuclear weapons and which believes it must do so. The Treaty is perfectly open about this. Article X states:

"Each Party shall in exercising its national sovereignty have the right to withdraw from the Treaty if it decides that extraordinary events, related to the subject matter of this Treaty, have jeopardised the supreme interests of its country. It shall give notice of such withdrawal to all other Parties to the Treaty and to the United Nations Security

---

* Natural uranium is 99·3 per cent Uranium 238 and only 0·7 per cent Uranium 235.

Council three months in advance. Such notice shall include a statement of the extraordinary events it regards as having jeopardised its supreme interests."

This clause follows essentially the same wording as Article IV of the partial nuclear test ban:

"This treaty shall be of unlimited duration. Each party shall, in exercising its national sovereignty, have the right to withdraw from the treaty if it decides that extraordinary events, related to the subject matter of this treaty, have jeopardised the supreme interests of its country. It shall give notice of such withdrawal to all other parties to the treaty three months in advance."

These articles help to avoid the familiar errors of lawyers in interpreting treaties with security implications. The decision to spend substantial resources on developing nuclear weapons is a serious and important one for a government to take. Even without the escape clause, it would not have been inhibited by treaties entered into many years before by other governments in other circumstances—treaties which, incidentally, have a markedly unequal character. This fact will not be lost on any government which finds it necessary to denounce one or both of these treaties in future years.

Unfortunately, the recognition in these treaties of the reality of sovereign states responsible for their own security has not been extended to the safeguards systems. Plutonium-producing facilities have been built in many countries on the assumption that undertakings to use the resulting materials only for peaceful purposes are adequate. Governments that believe this are believing that other governments—over long periods of time, through new regimes and in new circumstances—will be inhibited from developing weapons from plutonium which they have paid for, which they own, and which is within their sovereign territory. The governments of most of the leading industrial powers profess to believe this extraordinary position: and they base their actions on it. They stand ready to build nuclear reactors throughout the world and to provide the necessary fuels. In two notable cases, reactors were built without even nominal restrictions on the plutonium produced from them: the

French reactor at Dimona, in Israel, and the Canadian one at Trombay, in India. In the Canadian case, there was an undertaking that the plutonium produced would be used for peaceful purposes only: no undertakings are known to have been associated with the Dimona facility. India was able to produce and fabricate her own uranium fuel rods from her own resources for Trombay and has built a chemical separation plant for the plutonium (which is based on equipment bought in both Britain and the United States without any restrictions). Israel has had a greater problem of fuel supplies but has largely solved this by developing uranium production as a by-product of the Dead Sea phosphate industry.

These two examples have caused great concern to the major powers, and with reason. The weakness of the Indian undertaking to Canada was clearly illustrated by the claims of the Indian Prime Minister, Mr. Nehru, on a number of occasions that India could produce nuclear weapons in a period of 18 months. This statement was based on the assumption that the Trombay plutonium would be used. Since then, however, major reactors have been built in India by both the United States and Canada under various complex agreements providing for various forms of inspection of the plutonium produced. Canada is also building a major reactor in Pakistan; Britain has done so in Italy and Japan; the United States has in West Germany, Japan and a number of other countries; West Germany is building one in Argentina; France has built one in Spain. It may be doubted whether any of these facilities is providing electricity more cheaply than it might have been obtained from other sources. It is the habit of governments to justify uneconomic nuclear facilities by the argument that other and subsequent nuclear power production will be economic. The strong commercial reasons for this have found in the safeguards system an ideal barrier with which to resist the political concern which should be bearing on their activities. Almost without exception, the governments of the industrial countries capable of proliferating these facilities rely on the argument that if they do not do it someone else will. There is no centre of power or effective coalition in the world which is adequate to build the common policy which can restrain this dangerous competition.

Of the 140-odd states, five have so far embarked on the construction of nuclear weapons. These are the United States, which exploded a device in 1945, the Soviet Union (1949), Britain (1952), France (1960) and the People's Republic of China (1964). Canada and Sweden could have produced nuclear explosives but have not thought it worth the economic and political costs. The Federal Republic of Germany and Japan could now do so quite rapidly but have chosen on political grounds to restrain themselves. In the German case, there are strong inhibitions caused by the country's military vulnerability unless the other N.A.T.O. powers (led by the United States) are prepared to give their support to the programme. This sense of military immediacy is also present in the Israeli debate, where it is argued that a weapons programme which had not yet borne fruit could be exceptionally dangerous.* Israel is the first example of a country which could not produce nuclear weapons from its own resources but which has been provided with most of the difficult elements of plutonium production by the major powers.

It may be assumed that the Israeli case will be repeated in many countries—subject to the qualification that the plutonium will be under international inspection of one kind or another. We can therefore expect the number of countries able to build nuclear weapons to grow steadily. It would seem possible already to place Italy, Belgium, the Netherlands, Czechoslovakia† and East Germany† in this category. In the next decade another dozen countries can be expected to have the most difficult industrial elements in nuclear weapons construction solved for them by outsiders.

* This argument should also have been valid for a China under strong pressure from the United States, but it did not prove an impediment to the development of Chinese nuclear weapons.

† It appears that plutonium produced in the Soviet-built reactors in the Warsaw Pact countries is returned to the Soviet Union.

In the meantime, there is a growing and evident tendency to buy options so that a future decision to build national nuclear weapons can be taken if necessary. A number of countries, contemplating the uncertain world in which they live, are deliberately providing themselves with some of the facilities they will need if they decide to build nuclear weapons. Possible future security needs are a common source of industrial effort in many countries in such fields as chemicals, optics, shipbuilding, aircraft, and so on: this tendency to acquire industries with potential security value is now discernible for the elements which are necessary to nuclear explosives. The most obvious (and least surprising) acquisition of an option has been in the Federal Republic of Germany, where all the significant facilities for plutonium production, uranium enrichment and advanced rocket development are being developed. The same can be said of Japan, though she does not yet have quite the same broad industrial strength to bring to bear. Other countries where the industrial options on nuclear explosives are being acquired are India, Pakistan and Australia. With every year, the governments of these countries will be able to acquire nuclear explosives in a shorter time and at a smaller price. For some, notably India and Pakistan, there is no very obvious way to acquire an effective nuclear delivery system. Israel and Australia, however, have procured high-performance aircraft from the United States that are easily adaptable to the nuclear strike role. If what is required is a powerful modern missile force, the only visible options at this point are the rocket programmes of Japan and West Germany. Whether others (such as Australia) would be in a position to buy an effective system from others remains to be seen. The only country that has sought to buy a nuclear delivery system from others, the United Kingdom, has been able to buy the finest American equipment. Indeed, the United States sought to repeat the same arrangements with France but was rebuffed. Though it is assumed to be out of the question, it is quite possible that new nuclear powers with a good relationship to a major power will be able to buy what they want when they want it. The fact that France is producing major

military systems—land-based and submarine-based rockets—
in parallel with the United States augurs well for any
reasonably pro-western nascent nuclear power with cash
to offer.* The conventional arms problem has shown how
difficult it is to maintain what amounts to arms embargoes
in a competitive situation.

This said, it is nevertheless clear that the growth of
nuclear options will be very uneven, conferring very differing
possibilities on the countries of the world. So will the acquisition of the weapons themselves. This is already evident in the
great difference in the nuclear forces of the five existing
nuclear powers. If Israel, India, Australia or Japan exercised
the options they are acquiring, they would be very different
again: and the smaller powers that might follow would
illustrate many different types of nuclear power. The
American strategic community, which has tended to give
the lead on this subject, has always shown a contradictory
fear of the spread of nuclear weapons in general and a
particular contempt for any nuclear force that is not large
and invulnerable. It is assumed that the mathematical
perfection which is sought in the American force—and
assumed, not always with justification, in the Soviet Union—
is the only realistic† kind of nuclear power. The reality is
much less tidy than this and will be very untidy indeed if
present trends continue. Small countries have a few ships
which great navies would regard as an unbalanced fleet
unable to operate effectively; their armies are half equipped;
their weapons do not properly form themselves around a
coherent tactical doctrine. They buy what they can afford
and employ the doctrines that come the way of their staff
officers. When a political or military crisis occurs, the

---

* Students of actual behaviour rather than declaratory policy will do
well to note the case of the French *force de frappe*, which the United
States Government consistently and openly opposed. This opposition
nevertheless found room for the offer of Polaris missiles at Nassau in
December, 1962, on the same terms as to Britain, and the provision of
KC–135 tankers which gave the first stage of the *force de frappe* (Mirage
4 bombers) the range to reach the Soviet Union.

† Such words as meaningful, viable and valid are used in this context.

politicians do what lies in their power. However unintelligible to the strategic thinkers of the great powers, this is the way most of the world is run. It is the context in which nuclear proliferation will take place.

Far the most important element of nuclear proliferation at present and for the next few years is the spread of plutonium stocks to many countries as a by-product of electric power production or the desalination of sea water in nuclear reactors. The American, British, Canadian, French, German and Swedish atomic energy industries are all eager to sell such facilities to virtually any countries that will buy. (Soviet intentions are more obscure outside the Warsaw Pact area.) Present policies seem to imply that plutonium stocks will come into existence in many jurisdictions. This will be a simple physical fact. It will be modified by a political environment consisting of inspectors, usually from the International Atomic Energy Agency. It has already been argued that these political and legal facts are entirely inadequate to the control of the physical realities.

The Baruch Plan of 1946 was based on the technical belief of the time that certain forms of plutonium—basically, that which has been left in reactors for a substantial period—were valueless for weapons. It was assumed at that time that plutonium stocks could safely grow around the world provided they were not of weapons grade. The metal would have no more value to bomb makers than natural uranium. The changes of technology have unfortunately withdrawn this favourable fact. It seems that a quarter of a century of further development has left little doubt that virtually all plutonium is of value for weapons, though some is greatly to be preferred to others.

However, there may be limits to the power of a nuclear force built on plutonium. Countries building thermonuclear weapons, or hydrogen bombs, seem invariably to have built the fusion weapon around a fission bomb using enriched uranium rather than plutonium. For a time it was suggested that a hydrogen bomb could not be made from plutonium: and whether or not this is strictly true it seems that the operation is very difficult and largely impracticable. Although the fate of Nagasaki is dramatic evidence of the power of a basic plutonium device,* this would suggest that a world of plutonium stocks does not create world-wide options on thermonuclear weapons.†

Enriched uranium is therefore the most important material for large nuclear weapons. When the problem of building these explosives was first examined seriously in 1940 and 1941, it was realized that there were two possible solutions: to produce the new element (later called plutonium) in a reactor; or to separate out the one part in 140 in natural uranium which was Uranium 235. This second line of development led to the Hiroshima bomb and has been the source of the thermonuclear weapons on which the heavy nuclear forces have been based.

Uranium 235 and Uranium 238 are chemically identical, their only important difference being that U-235 is slightly lighter. If they are put into a gaseous form (uranium hexafluoride, a notoriously difficult material, is apparently the only usable compound for this purpose) the molecules containing U-235 have a higher average speed than those containing U-238, the gravitational pull on them is slightly less, and in certain conditions the electric, magnetic,

---

* The bomb dropped on Nagasaki had a yield of approximately 20 kilotons. Standard French plutonium bombs, illustrated in even their earliest tests, have three times this power.

† Sir John Cockcroft, who played a central part in the British nuclear weapons programme as director of the Atomic Energy Research Establishment, Harwell, wrote the following just before his death in 1967: "There is good evidence that the nations concerned have found that, while pure fission bombs (A-bombs) can be made using either uranium–235 or plutonium, a military practicable fusion bomb (H-bomb) requires uranium–235 for the fission trigger.' *Unless Peace Comes*, ed, by Nigel Calder (London, Penguin, 1968 and New York, Viking).

In the same remarkable volume, Dr. David Inglis, a senior physicist at the Argonne National Laboratory, Chicago, writes: "In practice, a uranium–235 bomb serves as the 'trigger' to create the very high temperature and detonate the fusible material of the H-bomb" (p. 52). However, he suggests that things could change. "Less improbable, perhaps, is the eventual design of efficient H-bombs using a plutonium trigger if, indeed, present H-bomb triggers are essentially uranium–235, as is suggested by Sir John Cockcroft in the previous chapter." (p. 59.)

inter-atomic or inter-molecular forces can be different. Anyone wanting to enrich uranium —that is, to increase its proportion of U-235—must exploit one of these differences on an
industrial scale. It seems that for weapons a proportion of
U-235 in excess of 90 per cent is necessary. While nuclear
reactors have spread, with their by-product of plutonium,
this uranium enrichment technology has remained obdur-
ately difficult, exceedingly expensive and in decisive respects
secret.

Seven ways in which the differences between U-235 and
U-238 might be exploited to separate them presented themselves in the early days of the Manhattan Project in the
United States. Only four, however, seemed suitable for
uranium separation and they were all tried between 1941
and 1945. Of one of these, liquid thermal separation, little
has been heard since. That leaves three: gaseous diffusion,
electromagnetism and the gas centrifuge. The gas centrifuge
was also dropped in the wartime programme but has since
re-emerged. The electromagnetic method yielded some
results; but the great success of the gaseous diffusion method
in the American programme established it as the classic
method and it has been used by the United States itself, the
Soviet Union, Britain, France and China (though China is a
special case). While successful, this method has been extremely difficult and costly. Enrichment is only possible on a
large scale; the development problems for the barrier with
billions of microscopic holes through which the gas must
pass were still very difficult for the French in the 1960s;
and the electric power consumption is immense. No one
has seriously contemplated building such a plant except
as part of a major nuclear weapons programme. It is not
something that is acquired nominally for other reasons but
partially as an option on a future nuclear weapons programme. Options at prices ranging up to $1,000,000,000 do
not command a ready market, especially when they are not
easily explained away with the euphemisms of atoms for
peace, ploughshares rather than swords, or peaceful exploration of space.

Uranium enrichment has been the steep escarpment to be

scaled in both the French and Chinese nuclear weapon programmes. Their positions were different and so were their solutions. The French decided to build a conventional gaseous diffusion plant at Pierrelatte of the relatively small size built by the British at Capenhurst but of considerably higher quality. This took them some years longer than they had expected, seriously delaying their first H-bomb test; and it cost them the $1,000,000,000 (approximately) that the Americans had paid for their first plant.* The French Government's public difficulties in this matter may have induced others to hesitate.

The orthodox American view, which there is no reason to doubt, is that the Russians built a standard Soviet-type gaseous diffusion plant in China as part of a general development of the Chinese nuclear industry. This plant (it is believed) is incomplete if part of a military programme, though not as part of a civil programme. The reason for this is that it will enrich uranium up to the 5 per cent U-235 which is commonly used as fuel for nuclear reactors; but there is no way of continuing up to the 90 per cent or more for weapons. It is not difficult to speculate on the kind of negotiations which this project provoked between Moscow and Peking. What appears to have happened, however, is that the Chinese turned to the electromagnetic process to complete the enrichment.†

These two examples, the most recent available, suggest that the problem of uranium enrichment remains formidable. As long as gaseous diffusion holds the field, this is likely to remain true. There is, however, a serious challenger to

* The value of money had, of course, diminished considerably in the interim, which no doubt accounts for the comparable cost for a considerably smaller facility.

† See Walter C. Clemens, Jr., "The Arms Race and Sino-Soviet Relations", The Hoover Institution on War, Revolution and Peace, Stanford, Calif., 1968, p. 23: "The first stage of the enrichment process was almost certainly carried out in the gaseous diffusion plant in Lanchow; this concentration was probably taken a step further by an electromagnetic process." He states that the electromagnetic process might have been developed by the Chinese from blue prints declassified by the United States in 1955 and the Soviet Union in 1958.

gaseous diffusion in the high-speed centrifuge being developed in the United States, the Netherlands, West Germany, Britain, Japan and Australia, at least. It appears that
this process has considerable advantages for those seeking an
option on the production of weapons-grade enriched
uranium. The development is being promoted in certain
countries—West Germany, Japan, Australia—which are
clearly interested in such an option. All those involved
in the development of the gas centrifuge method are, of
course, together in claiming as their sole purpose the acquisition of a cheaper method of enriching uranium as fuel for
reactors. Some, notably the Europeans, also argue that
they are determined to free themselves from dependence
on the goodwill of the possessors of gaseous diffusion
plants for their supplies of fuel in the future. The non-
weapons case is persuasive enough to have attracted the
British Government (which not only has a gaseous diffusion
plant but has acquired American enriched uranium in
exchange for plutonium) and also the Netherlands
Government, which shows no sign of interest in a nuclear
option.

There is a high degree of confidence that three or four years
of vigorous development by a substantial industrial power
will make the centrifuge method economical. If this is
correct, and if the technology is not restricted closely, the
means of uranium enrichment could spread widely in the
coming years. The export policies of those countries or
groups of countries which develop the centrifuge will, of
course, make a very great difference. Clearly, they will
export enriched uranium for reactor purposes, and though
it is generally believed that this raises no serious proliferation
problems, the Chinese weapons programme may force a
revision of this view. Another decisive issue is the export
policy for the centrifuges themselves. Any country or group
of countries going to the expense of developing this process
and setting up a factory for producing centrifuges will be
strongly tempted to export them. Cascades of centrifuges
designed for the low enrichment stages can apparently be
reorganized to achieve the high enrichment stages. Even a

small centrifuge facility could therefore be the foundation of a national nuclear weapons programme.

These political and military dangers are not impeding centrifuge development. After years of working in total secrecy, the British Government has made a joint and public arrangement to develop and sell centrifuges. The Anglo-Dutch-German trio show every determination to sell not only enriched uranium but the centrifuges themselves to others, probably subject to the qualification that the recipient must have signed the N.P.T. The British have shown their thinking on this (admittedly in a specially intimate relationship) by offering the Australians a centrifuge facility as part of a long-term reactor agreement. Japanese efforts are equally likely to be vigorous and unrestricted. The United States has not fought these trends and shows signs of anxiety only about letting others take the leadership in economical uranium enrichment. There is no sign anywhere of an anti-proliferation policy working to restrain governments in this field. As with reactors, those who are politically concerned are unable to propose a policy which sounds realistic. Such inhibitions as there were have been removed by the promise of safeguards and by signatures of the Non-Proliferation Treaty.

The economics may yet, of course, prove unattractive. American stocks of enriched uranium are such that the United States can lower the price as she chooses, at least for the immediate future; and her production capacity in her three gaseous diffusion plants is such that even at higher costs she would be highly competitive with a method which must still be developed and tooled up for centrifuge production before the centrifuge plants themselves can be built. This very fact of an effective American monopoly backed by substantial economic and political power is, however, one of the main incentives to other governments to make a reality of gas centrifuge uranium enrichment. If the centrifuge party proves to be right and they can show competitive costs, the great barrier to the proliferation of thermonuclear weapons will have been breached. This prospect is causing no visible concern to any of those engaged in the breaching operation.

The effects of nuclear proliferation are not predictable or quantifiable. There may be some rigid almost mathematical structure which has fastened itself on to the great fleet of Soviet and American strategic missiles. That structure may indeed stretch right down to all the other nuclear explosives in their possession—apart from any that might be stolen or be subject to some kind of accident. British nuclear weapons may be caught up in this, at least for the present. One can make one's own assessment about the French and Chinese. But states are not units on a board. They are artifices held together by force or consent, liable to unite with others, break up, be seized or be swept into some chaotic situation of which the government understands little. Nuclear weapons, or indeed a plutonium stockpile, are in a particular place under the control of particular men. More of them means more places, more men and different men. They will be dealt with according to the judgement of these men as to what the effects will be. Certain obvious dangers can be identified: a local nuclear arms race where the side which arrives first has a unique incentive to use its advantages; a civil war where a stock of nuclear weapons becomes important: a straightforward use of nuclear weapons at a bitter stage of a local war; the disappearance of a stock of plutonium,* enriched uranium or fabricated bombs into the hands of organized groups who cannot be deterred by threats of retaliation because they have no territory.

The structure being created to control proliferation will not control it. What it is doing, however, is to lift the political restraints from the commercial and industrial forces working to spread the essential technology and materials. There should be no illusions about the consequences, even though these will show themselves only gradually over the years.

---

* This has apparently already happened to a small quantity of plutonium in Argentina. It has never been found.

III   *Accident and civil war*

With nuclear weapons now distributed in very large numbers
especially in the American and Russian armed forces, the
dangers of accidental or unauthorized use are obvious. They
have been a favourite topic for fiction. Throughout history,
sovereigns and governments have always had the problem
of ensuring that their military servants obeyed their wishes.
In recent years, this problem has been mitigated by means
of communication which enable detailed direction to be
maintained from the centre. At the same time, the consequences of indiscipline or technical accident have become
far graver.

Where nuclear explosives themselves are concerned, the
nature of the critical mass which causes the explosion is such
that arming the weapon can be made a decisive and positive
series of actions. The fact that American nuclear weapons
are kept unarmed is best demonstrated by the 15 or more air
crashes involving nuclear weapons. None has resulted in a
nuclear explosion, though in many cases there has been a
release of radioactive materials. The development of electronic locks, which make a weapon unusable until a coded
signal has been passed through it, has given the authorities
at the centre (in the United States, at any rate) the ability
to withhold all initiative from their servants if they choose.
The extent to which this is used has never been published;
but the planners must be careful not to hold so much authority at the centre that the entire system can be neutralized
by destroying the centre. It seems reasonable to conclude
that the chances of technical accident are very small, though
they obviously exist; and the chances of unauthorized use
might be somewhat greater if likely motives can be imagined.
An insane desire to see the world destroyed is a common
motive among the fiction writers; but while it seems to lack
conviction, the same cannot necessarily be said of deeply
felt political motives. A Hungarian in 1956, for example, a
Jordanian in 1967, a Czech in 1968, or an Ibo in 1969 might
have been moved to an unauthorized use of a nuclear weapon

if he had had one under his control. Actions of this kind would be very much more likely between the present nuclear powers in a period of conventional conflict which aroused deep-seated bitterness.

Once all possible precautions have been taken, there is little that can be said or done about accidents and unauthorized actions. They are in the nature of things unpredictable and accidental. The important thing is that power should be so organized that an accident of this kind would not provoke disastrous consequences. Here once more the key to the problem is the secure second strike system. If a power feels the kind of conviction about the invulnerability of its retaliatory forces which the United States felt between 1962 and 1967 (for example), it will feel no need to respond uncontrollably to an isolated attack. It will be prepared to investigate and enquire. There will be no question of firing weapons on the basis of radar warning; and no response will be allowed to be automatic. All these practices have grown and prospered in the United States in recent years. They are not the sign of a new enlightenment: they are a direct result of a nuclear force which can be seen by everyone to be secure. By contrast, a force which knows itself to be fully targeted by the other side will rely on technical uncertainties, strategic warning and immediate response to maintain a continuing deterrent. The deterrent might well be there: but it is accompanied by a proneness to disastrous accident. The best way for the powers to deal with the accidental and unauthorized use of weapons is to remove all possibility that nuclear delivery systems—their own or others'—might be vulnerable. They also need the machinery which will see that in an unforeseen situation in which control might be lost the common interest in preventing further disintegration is turned into effective action.

The problem of civil war is in a sense an extension of the problem of the unauthorized use of nuclear weapons. In the end, authority and sovereignty in nation states rest with those who control effective power: and there is no evidence about how effective nuclear power would be in a civil war. Do these weapons so strengthen the power of the established authorities that rebellion in a nuclear power is excluded? Or, on the contrary, do they enable a handful of air force or army commanders to dictate to an existing government? The three original nuclear powers—the United States, the Soviet Union and Britain—have had such stable political systems in recent years that the question has not arisen. The same is not true of France, where the central government was effectively dominated by the army in 1958 and the army, renewing its revolt, was suppressed by the central government in 1960 after a tense period. Clearly, physical power has played an important part in the political life of France in the recent past and could easily do so again. It must be assumed that this will be true of many other countries. There is even some fear in the United States that their central institutions may once more force a challenge and there are those who foresee the possibility of revolution in the Soviet Union.

The part that nuclear weapons play in the internal political life of countries possessing them depends to a considerable extent on the type of nuclear weapons systems which are developed and the lengths to which revolutionaries might be prepared to go. Land-based systems, like Minuteman or the Soviet long-range air and rocket forces, could take part in a revolutionary situation only if they were used in a revolt which included substantial ground forces to provide for their protection. But while a lone revolution by a nuclear arm is no doubt out of the question, it is clear that an army revolt which included substantial numbers of nuclear weapons would be very difficult to handle. Missile-firing submarines introduce a new and baffling element into the situation. Their survival does not depend on the control of ground; and they represent a vast power of destruction without any ability to occupy ground in the hands of those who control them. Just who would control them in a civil war situation must be in doubt in any country. It is likely that in the United States, for example, some control will be outside the submarines with those who have been entrusted with certain coded signals. But this is not certain. All that is reliably known is that no order to launch an

American submarine-based missile can be given without the independent confirmation of the captain and first officer. Their loyalties, their knowledge, and many other factors would enter into the situation. Navies have not traditionally been the source of insurrection and rebellion, presumably because they have not been well-placed to challenge the authority of governments. It may be doubted whether sea-borne nuclear power will change this situation, but it introduces a remarkable new factor into any civil war situation. Both submarine-based and land-based nuclear weapons, whether missiles or bombers, appear to lack credibility for the early stages of a civil war situation simply because their effects are too awful. It is impossible to imagine French nuclear weapons being used against the revolting troops in 1960 or being used by the troops themselves against cities or loyal troops. On the other hand, the temptation to threaten may at times be irresistible and threats can involve men in actions they did not intend.

In most situations both governments and insurrectionary forces will be anxious to keep the nuclear weapons from being used. Nevertheless, if the conflict dragged on, the side which was losing might decide that possession of even a small batch of nuclear weapons would be enough to secure a section of the country and to deter the victors from destroying the last vestiges of their opposition. They might even feel obliged to make some limited use of the weapons to force the victorious army to recognize this threat. Such events do not sound so imaginary if one conceives of Spain as a nuclear power in 1936, China in 1948, Nigeria in 1967 or indeed any victim of a hard-fought civil war. Violent political change in a world of nuclear powers—even the present five—now involves this new range of risks.

IV   *New techniques of mass destruction*

Nuclear explosives are unique among weapons of mass destruction in the place they occupy in the organization of power in the world. This is not really surprising. Quite apart from their spectacular emergence at the end of the war which shaped the present world order, they remain uniquely precise, controllable and destructive. They also continue to yield technical possibilities which were previously doubted or disbelieved—as has been shown by the successful achievement of thermonuclear explosions and the extraordinary reductions in weight/yield ratios which have permitted multiple warheads. There is no immediate prospect of their displacement from the centre of attention in the present great powers.

It is clear, however, that great advances are being made in the control of the environment and that science is opening up a new range of weapons possibilities. The most important of these, nerve gases, derives from the Second World War but were not used then and have not been used since. New advances in both chemical and microbiological weapons are closely related to the improved understanding of human biology. Other more vast possibilities through environmental control and other techniques are now being seriously analysed and will come within the power of well-organized governments over the next few decades.

Chemical weapons in the form of incendiary bombs have already been used for mass destruction in the fire raids on Germany and Japan in 1945. The use of these weapons in war has a long history and toxic gases of various kinds were used against troops in the First World War, against civilians in Abyssinia and are widely used in various forms of riot control and internal security. Napalm has been employed extensively by the armed forces of the United States and is stocked as a standard weapon throughout the world. The possibility of really large-scale destructive power in gaseous weapons emerged with the German discovery of certain derivatives of phosphine oxide which were called Tabun, Sarin and Soman. These nerve gases can kill without being inhaled and are extremely lethal. New substances with the same effects have since been isolated and developed in the form of organophosphorus compounds. The way these things work is to inhibit the functioning of a particular enzyme without which the muscles and nerves cannot be controlled. They enter the body through the skin. The lethal dose of Sarin is about 0·7 milligrams but it will be absorbed in a few minutes if the concentration is between one tenth and three tenths of a milligram for each litre of air. Marcel Fetizon and Michel Magat estimate that "in order to reach a lethal concentration in the air of a city the size of Paris, to a height of about 15 metres, some 250 tons of Sarin would have to be distributed."* Such weapons would seem to be the beginning of a broad and expanding line of possibilities. These authors write:†

The further we go in our understanding of biochemical processes, the more possibilities for interference will develop. Modern medicine and biology are now making big strides in disentangling these life processes and we have already learned how to interfere with many of them—immune response (protection against infection), cell growth, cell division, etc. The discovery of 'messengers' regulating the production of specific enzymes indispensable for life processes gives new points of attack; so does the discovery of allostery—conformational changes of enzyme molecules induced by chemicals, which can enhance or reduce their activity.

These arguments apply equally to micro-biological agents, which are developing rapidly. Certain military difficulties remain with these weapons, as well as exceptionally powerful emotional inhibitions. Nevertheless, substantial sums are being spent in this field and it is being carried along on the back of medical and agricultural research.

Radiological weapons have been feared since the invention of nuclear weapons. These are radioactive agents continually giving off damaging radiation. It was felt by some people that they might be used by the Germans in defence of the Normandy beaches in 1944 and warnings were issued; General MacArthur proposed a vast belt of Cobalt 60, with its fatal gamma radiation, across Korea; and there have been rumours (unfounded) of Egyptian plans for radiological weapons for use against Israel. In fact, this class of weapon has basic weaknesses, the most fundamental of which is that

* *Unless Peace Comes*, ed. Nigel Calder (London, Penguin, and New York, Viking), p. 126.

† Ibid., p. 134.

it is extremely dangerous in the hands of those using it and must be heavily and expensively shielded. In storage it also gradually loses its effectiveness. As a dangerous element in the present system of power, these weapons are not worth extensive consideration.*

Environment control of various kinds is gradually coming within the power of men and could presumably be turned to military objectives. The most disturbing of these is the proposal, frequently discussed, for an agent which could temporarily absorb the ozone which lies in a layer in the atmosphere and absorbs most of the ultra-violet radiation from the sun. The removal of this layer from a particular area would have fatal results on unshielded life beneath.

Without pursuing any of these possibilities, it is clear that the advance of the biological and physical sciences can only have the effect of bringing new destructive means within the power of organized societies. The number of governments which will be able to make use of these powers will increase as wealth spreads and as discoveries become known. Some of these may be very much more ready than the major powers to embark on what would now be regarded as unorthodox weapons. There is always a tendency for the powerful and satisfied to become committed to the military means which gave them their powerful position. It is the outsider who is behind in these technologies who seeks out other possibilities. Great nuclear powers have a vested interest in making the most of the evidence of deficiencies in alternative weapons. They are receptive to the arguments (in themselves excellent) that such developments will be unpredictable and dangerous. Challenging powers may be less receptive to them. So may embattled governments faced with powerful neighbours, or even oppressed peoples trying to break the rule of a central order. Dangerous new weapons take a combination of

---

* This same conclusion has been reached by the Government of the Netherlands, which in a working paper to the Conference of the Committee on Disarmament concludes: "Judging by the available information possibilities for radiological warfare do exist theoretically, but do not seem to be of much or even of any practical significance." See Document CCD/291, 14 July 1970, Geneva.

physical possibility and political determination. The absence of the determination in the greatest and most satisfied powers will have a useful dampening effect on others but it may not be decisive. The more unexploited possibilities become available, the greater will be the temptations to the adventurer and the more difficult the problem of handling him.

V *Miscalculation*

The most serious single danger of the nuclear or conventional confrontations in the world is undoubtedly miscalculation. Here there is neither accident nor premeditated war. The authorities which control the armed forces of a country make certain moves on the assumptions that they will provoke certain responses and convey certain information: and these moves in fact convey very different information and bring about an unforeseen response. The German miscalculation about the possibility of American entry into the European wars of the twentieth century is an outstanding example of the consequences of making assumptions about uncommitted nations. Similarly, the North Koreans miscalculated the American and Western reaction to their invasion of South Korea in 1950 and the Allied high command subsequently miscalculated the Chinese reaction to their advances. Countries can miscalculate even those they know very well: the British and French made an important mistake in assessing the likely American reaction if they launched their Suez invasion in 1956. They thought the United States Government would be compelled to support them. No one in the West knows what calculations can have gone into the Russian decision to introduce missiles into Cuba in 1962, but it seems reasonable to assume that they misread the probable American response.

Uncertain commitments provide the most fertile ground for miscalculation. The Russians may miscalculate what the Americans, British and French would do if they cut off the road into Berlin; but they know that there is a strong commitment and any move they make is likely to be designed to test how the commitment would be implemented. But the Chinese could make a serious error over the extent of the American or Soviet commitment to India or the Americans a similar error over the nature of the Russian commitment to China, especially at a time of Sino-Soviet conflict. The American refusal to support the Anglo-French Suez expedition might have been thought to show a complete disengagement from the consequences. But when the Russians issued their rocket threats, the Americans found that they had to reassert the commitment. This could have been the basis for a serious Soviet miscalculation.

The only solution to this perennial problem is that commitments should be as clear-cut as possible and that as much prior thinking and planning as possible should take place. To avoid making mistakes, each side needs to have a detailed grasp of the military and political objectives of the other. The publication of large amounts of testimony about weapons and objectives of the United States Government undoubtedly helps greatly in the education of the Soviet government machine about the military assumptions of the West. Their political knowledge and the West's military and political knowledge depend on the quality of the intelligence services, which are the main weapon in the avoidance of miscalculation.

VI   *The involvement of the major powers in local conflicts*

One of the central dangers in the balance of terror, as at present established, is the possibility that revolution, subversion or local aggression elsewhere in the world will draw the major powers in. This is the classic form of escalation as represented, in particular, by the rapid enlargement of the conflict between Serbia and Austria-Hungary in 1914. The nuclear powers have been drawn into local situations in Korea, Hungary, Egypt, the Lebanon, Jordan, Cuba, Malaysia, Vietnam, Czechoslovakia and elsewhere in recent years; and they have sent the forces of neutrals (or as near neutrals as they could get) under the United Nations banner into Gaza, the Congo, Cyprus and other situations so as to reduce the danger of a direct confrontation among themselves. Only in Hungary, where the Americans held back, and in Cuba, where the Russians showed extreme caution when challenged, did American–Russian or allied–Russian conflict seem a possibility. At the risk of broad generalization, it might be said that all the conflicts so far have been resolved on the broad assumption that the Russians are a mainly European power; and this assumption has been just true enough for the system to have worked. If the Russians decide at some point to extend their military power overseas much more dangerous conflicts could result. The pressure on Western governments to do nothing, as in Hungary, would be very strong on military grounds; but on political grounds abstention in the event of strong Russian interest would be exceptionally difficult for the West.

Even in the present situation, a great deal of diplomatic effort and skill is devoted to the problem of acting effectively without coming into conflict. The United States and the Soviet Union must find a tacit agreement on fundamentals in all situations. This process is largely a matter of unilateral assertion, taking account of the probable response of the other side. It also has severe limits, especially from the point of view of the West. The direct involvement of the N.A.T.O. powers in Cyprus in 1964 gave the Soviet Union a strong incentive to avoid the appeal for aid which Archbishop Makarios extended. In a reverse situation, the opposite would probably not have been the case. The involvement of the Soviet Union or its satellites would have made American abstention more difficult.

Clearly, the only hope of a prolonged avoidance of great power conflict in the third world is the development of a body of clearly understood rules of action. The only important rule which now commands even nominal acceptance is that aggression—the actual crossing of borders by troops—is improper. Even this rule has regularly been broken by those who subscribe to it: the Russians in Hungary and Czechoslovakia, the Americans in Cambodia, the British and French at Suez, the Indians at Goa, the Indonesians in Malaysia, the Israelis around their borders. In each case it has been argued that an intolerable situation had been created by internal occurrences in the other state. Special situations producing serious crises involving the nuclear powers have been generated by a Soviet threat to sign a peace treaty with East Germany (which would have compelled the Allied occupation powers in Berlin to negotiate their rights of access with a government they did not recognize), the stationing of Russian missiles in Cuba (which the American President said he considered to be in itself an act of aggression, thus emptying the word of any strict and technical meaning it might have), the civil war in Cyprus and the detachment of Katanga from the Congo.

Although operations have frequently been undertaken by major powers in support of the interests of smaller allies, there has not so far been an intervention by the United States and the Soviet Union on opposite sides. In any intervention, there is a complex problem of control over the situation with a natural difference between the great patron and the passions of the smaller power (given additional strength by the accession of great power support). The strains have been evident in each of these situations. Perhaps the most spectacular example was the release of the North Korean prisoners by Synghman Rhee in 1953 at a time when the fate of these prisoners was believed to be critical to the peace which the United States and her allies had so arduously negotiated. The American troubles with the Government of South Vietnam are well known; those of Britain with the Malaysian Government less so. The Russians never fail to warn the West of the difficulties it will face in controlling West Germany in any conflict. They themselves may still be the guarantors of a China they not only cannot control but with which they are in bitter and protracted conflict. There is a natural tendency for those in a local conflict to exploit every weapon available to win it. There is an equal need for the major powers—especially when they have placed themselves on opposite sides—to ensure that they are not drawn into a situation which works against their primary need for a basic world order. Germany understood this difficulty and built her policy on it in the tense years up to 1914 when Austria–Hungary was trying to involve her in the Balkan problem. Her Emperor forgot it in his anger at the shocking assassination of Sarajevo. This tension between the major powers and the local powers is inevitable and imposes a complexity on policy which in other cases besides that of Kaiser Wilhelm II might prove too much for politicians in power.

*　　*　　*

The present structure of power cannot therefore be relied on indefinitely. Certain elements in it—the destabilizing progress of nuclear technology, the spread of nuclear weapons, the development of microbiological weapons—demand early action and will become harder to solve if time is lost. The period of second-strike nuclear weapons systems and the parallel period of a widespread anxiety among the middle powers to avoid the need to acquire nuclear weapons may be unrepeatable. The choice may not be a new world order or war: but it may be a new world order now or a very much less satisfactory one many years from now. Because of these weaknesses, the case for the *status quo* does not seem to be as strong as is generally assumed by governments.

3

THE PLANS FOR REFORM

GOVERNMENTS have for many years sought means of reducing what they conceived to be excessive levels of armaments. Frequently they have argued that this would increase security by removing tension and the prospect of war; and they have invariably been attracted by the hope of a general reduction in expenditure on armed forces.

Periods of disarmament are sometimes rapid and dramatic and sometimes gradual and imperceptible. The most striking disarmament usually follows the political resolution of war; and rearmament is common when unresolved problems are growing more severe and bargaining is becoming more intense. It can be assumed that success in solving political problems will lead to lower levels of armaments all round. But traditional disarmament goes beyond the creation of a political context in which arms appear less urgent to governments. It sets out to reduce arms by agreement among rival powers on three assumptions: that arms themselves tend to heighten rivalry; that at lower levels of forces there would be a smaller chance of war; and that if war broke out it would be less severe. Reducing arms in this way means assuring each side that the other is fulfilling its obligations. It also means searching for means of reduction which all sides will see to be equitable. This raises serious difficulties. Even if military men can be brought to equate weapons, powers of growing importance will almost invariably consider that any disarmament scheme discriminates against them while predominant powers being challenged by others are unlikely to concede a parity which is not yet proved. This was a major problem of disarmament negotiations in the inter-war period; it showed itself in the 1946 American–

Soviet nuclear negotiations; and it can be anticipated with, for example, new nuclear powers.

The difficulties of partial disarmament in the present world are exceptionally great. While it is very difficult to argue that there is any such thing as equality in armaments today at any level, the makers of disarmament plans are expected to produce it for the ends of their various stages. To talk about equality in divisions in 1914 was just possible, though geography and other factors introduced important complications. But equality in that sense is now a thing of the past, with strategies which assume the use of different kinds of weapons at different times and with types of weapons which are so varied as to be impossible to compare. Formal disarmament thinking has had to struggle with these difficulties and has been attracted to such notions as freezes in existing weapons, proportionate reductions and ceilings on particular types of forces or global items such as manpower or defence budgets.

Because of the complexity of the military arguments, and for other less identifiable reasons, the old idea of cutting forces back on an agreed basis under control and inspection gave way in the late 1950s to general and complete disarmament (G.C.D.). It was argued that, once achieved, this would give equality to the great and the small, the rising and the declining, the nuclear and the non-nuclear. If there was to be security or insecurity, all at least would share it alike.

Both as a negotiating stance and as a long-term dream, general and complete disarmament has enjoyed remarkable success. In the early 1960s it dominated disarmament negotiations; and though the evident distaste of a number of governments for the idea led for a time to a concentration on other issues, it has not been formally abandoned. Indeed, the beginning of the 1970s brought it back into official discussions. The Italian Government showed great anxiety that further work should be done in this field and invited a group of nations to work out joint proposals. U Thant, the Secretary-General of the United Nations, consistently sustained this notion, as did General Assembly security resolutions. U Thant's speech of 22 May 1970, is typical: "The world stands at a most critical crossroads. It must halt and reverse the mad momentum of the nuclear arms race and move ahead towards the goal of general and complete disarmament, or the outlook for humankind is black indeed." The Soviet Union has consistently taken a position of strong support for general disarmament. On 16 June 1970, the leader of its delegation to the Conference of the Committee on Disarmament, Mr. A. A. Roschin, proposed that negotiations should begin again on this subject. "In proposing the reactivation at the present time of discussions on general and complete disarmament the Soviet Union proceeds from the premise that as a result of the conclusion of agreements on certain partial measures of disarmament a useful amount of experience has been acquired for continuing talks on problems of disarmament and the necessary organizational forums for such talks have been established." Responding a week later, the acting head of the United Nations delegation, Ambassador James F. Leonard, put the public American position: "I want to make it clear at the outset that we continue to support the goal of general and complete disarmament. At the same time, however, I think that all of us will agree that progress towards general and complete disarmament cannot be made in a vacuum but will have to be accompanied by concrete progress towards a peaceful world."

In formal disarmament negotiations of this kind, then, we have been in the era of G.C.D. for nearly a decade. Under one definition or another, it is the official objective of almost all governments and of the United Nations. Although there is no evidence that any government's military advisers believe that such a scheme would add to national security, heads of most governments and their foreign ministers habitually say that this is their objective.

One need be neither a cynic nor a sceptic to say that in real policy terms these statements are nearly always untrue or at least misleading. Most governments do not want anything remotely like general and complete disarmament; and though they console themselves with the argument that in a better political climate some such thing might be desirable, it may be seriously doubted whether the most optimistic projections of the most favourable political developments over a century would produce political conditions in which they would accept the international anarchy that the pure notion of general and complete disarmament would produce.

In fact, no existing proposal for general and complete disarmament is directed towards what those words in their plain connotation would appear to imply. All stop short of abolishing arms at a point where a very considerable capacity to threaten, kill and dominate by military means still exists in the hands of governments. What is generally meant is either a drastic reduction of the amounts of arms in the world or the concentration of them into a single centre of world authority. These approaches (which broadly correspond to the Soviet and American approaches respectively) are fundamentally different in political character and objective. They have in common, however, the dismantling of the main armaments and the disbandment of most national armed forces. This massive disarmament is of itself regarded as a primary objective and it is assumed that it will serve the interests of all.

The idea that everyone would be safe if there were far fewer engines of war is scarcely surprising in itself. Most people feel that if these things exist they have some chance of being used. If they do not exist, they cannot be used. On the other hand, in most older countries and some new ones there is also a powerful sentiment of identification with the armed forces. People associate their security with a Navy (as in Britain or Japan) or an Army (as in France, Israel, or the Soviet Union) or even a Strategic Air Command (as in the United States in recent years); and these agents of power and destruction become the object of affection and a sense of security. The means of power are not by any means necessarily the object of universal fear and dislike. Where they have provided protection (or are thought to have), they attract strong loyalty and it is only with the utmost reluctance that public opinion will agree that they should be dismantled.

The special belief in disarmament as the central aim has deep and historic roots, but its appeal seems to have been strongest and most profound to those whose view of the world was shaped by the experience of the First World War. In Europe between 1914 and 1918 power seemed to have subjected policy to itself: armies destroyed each other and everything else within range with no very obvious purpose. Political objectives were more apparent in the Second World War. They have been clearer still in the exceptional care and restraint with which power has been used in the generation since 1945. It is not surprising, therefore, that there is a discernible falling off in the public passion for disarmament as such. There is undoubtedly a general anxiety on economic and financial grounds to cut back the resources which go into armed forces. This is felt particularly in the poorer countries and is a prominent theme in the United Nations. But as the sole way of achieving security, disarmament no longer stirs the passion it once did. To suggest this is not to argue the rightness or wrongness of general and complete disarmament; it is merely to suggest the time has passed when governments are obliged by public opinion to support disarmament proposals for their own sake.

The assumption which underlies the notion of G.C.D. is that arms exist because other arms exist. If one weapon can be abolished on one side, it may be assumed in principle that another will be freed for abolition on the other side. The scheme can be complicated by the existence of more than two rivals but the same principles apply; and disarmament negotiations have important blocs, even when everyone knew that a high proportion of existing forces and armaments would be maintained even if one or other of the super-powers disarmed completely.

The McCloy–Zorin Principles

General and complete disarmament is laid down as the joint Russo–American objective in a remarkable document called the "Joint Statement by the United States and the U.S.S.R. of Agreed Principles for Disarmament Negotiations, 20th

77

September 1961", which is generally known as the McCloy-Zorin principles. After a short introduction, it states:

The United States and the U.S.S.R. have agreed to recommend the following principles as the basis for future multilateral negotiations on disarmament and to call upon other states to co-operate in reaching early agreement on general and complete disarmament in a peaceful world in accordance with these principles.

1. The goal of negotiations is to achieve agreement on a programme which will ensure that (a) disarmament is general and complete and war is no longer an instrument for settling international problems, and (b) such disarmament is accompanied by the establishment of reliable procedures for the peaceful settlement of disputes and effective arrangements for the maintenance of peace in accordance with the principles of the United Nations Charter.

2. The programme for general and complete disarmament shall ensure that states will have at their disposal only those non-nuclear armaments, forces, facilities, and establishments as are agreed to be necessary to maintain internal order and protect the personal security of citizens; and that states shall support and provide agreed manpower for a United Nations peace force.

3. To this end, the programme for general and complete disarmament shall contain the necessary provisions, with respect to the military establishment for every nation, for:

(a) Disbanding of armed forces, dismantling of military establishments, including bases, cessation of the production of armaments as well as their liquidation or conversion to peaceful uses;

(b) Elimination of all stockpiles of nuclear, chemical, bacteriological, and other weapons of mass destruction and cessation of the production of such weapons;

(c) Elimination of all means of delivery weapons of mass destruction;

(d) Abolishment of the organization and institutions designed to organize the military effort of states, cessation of military training, and closing of all military training institutions;

(e) Discontinuance of military expenditures.

4. The disarmament programme should be implemented in an agreed sequence, by stages until it is completed, with each measure and stage carried out within specified time-limits. Transition to a subsequent stage in the process of disarmament should take place upon a review of the implementation of measures included in the preceding stage and upon a decision that all such measures have been implemented and verified and that any additional verification arrangements required for measures in the next stage are, when appropriate, ready to operate.

5. All measures of general and complete disarmament should be balanced so that at no stage of the implementation of the treaty could any state or group of states gain military advantage and that security is ensured equally for all.

6. All disarmament measures should be implemented from beginning to end under such strict and effective international control as would provide firm assurance that all parties are honouring their obligations. During and after the implementation of general and complete disarmament the most thorough control should be exercised, the nature and extent of such control depending on the requirements for verification of the disarmament measures being carried out in each stage. To implement control over and inspection of disarmament an International Disarmament Organization including all parties to the agreement should be created within the framework of the United Nations. This International Disarmament Organization and its inspectors should be assured unrestricted access without veto to all places as necessary for the purpose of effective verification.

7. Progress in disarmament should be accompanied by measures to strengthen institutions for maintaining peace and the settlement of international disputes by peaceful means. During and after the implementation of the programme of general and complete disarmament, there should be taken, in accordance with the principles of the United Nations Charter, the necessary measures to maintain international peace and security, including the obligation of states to place at the disposal of the United Nations agreed manpower necessary for an international peace force to be equipped with agreed types of armaments. Arrangements for the use of this force should ensure that the United Nations can effectively deter or suppress any threat or use of

arms in violation of the purposes and principles of the United Nations.

8. States participating in the negotiations should seek to achieve and implement the widest possible agreement at the earliest possible date. Efforts should continue without interruption until agreement upon the total programme has been achieved, and efforts to ensure early agreement on and implementation of measures of disarmament should be undertaken without prejudicing progress on agreement on the total programme and in such a way that these measures would facilitate and form part of that programme.

These principles were originally drawn up by the United States Government and accepted by the Soviets, subject to the elimination of one sentence from paragraph 6. This sentence read: "Such verification should ensure that not only agreed limitations or reductions take place but also that retained armed forces and armaments do not exceed agreed levels at any stage." This was the only central difference between Mr. Valerian Zorin, for the Soviet Government, and Mr. John J. McCloy, for the United States Government, for reasons explained by Mr. Zorin in a letter to Mr. McCloy: "While strongly advocating effective control over disarmament and wishing to facilitate as much as possible the achievement of agreement on this control, the Soviet Union is at the same time resolutely opposed to the establishment of control over armaments."

At certain points, the wording of the document conceals important differences between the two approaches. The most important difference is undoubtedly what is meant by "a United Nations peace force"—a matter on which the American and Russian positions are fundamentally at variance.

The importance of the McCloy–Zorin principles is that they establish the long-term objective of general and complete disarmament together with "reliable measures for the peaceful settlement of disputes". It is implied that the problem is merely one of finding the means of achieving these two things. But is this true? Is either side convinced that its

own plan, if perfectly enforced, would give it security?
There is no evidence that they are. Yet all disarmament
negotiations (and particularly the notion of G.C.D.) make
this assumption. Because of this, the powers are obliged to
conduct a continuous debate about a secondary problem—
the technicalities of inspection. Having committed themselves
to ends which are at variance with the established national
security policy of their countries, the disarmament delegations of each are under an obligation to find serious dis-
agreements about the means. Generally speaking, this has
not been difficult. The Russians constantly accuse the West
of wanting to use a disarmament agreement as a means of
breaking down Soviet secrecy and so of undermining the
security of the Soviet Union before there has been any disarmament. The West has a well-established position that
there can be no certainty that a reduction has been carried
out unless what exists after the reduction can be established.
Each side then suggests that technicalities such as these
are the main impediment to an almost total abolition of
arms.

One of the basic principles in the McCloy–Zorin formulation demands re-examination, especially since it has been
one of the working principles of all post-war disarmament
negotiations. Paragraph 5 makes it a pair of twin objectives
that "at no stage of the implementation of the treaty could
any state or group of states gain military advantage and that
security is ensured for all". The sentiments here are un-
exceptionable; and it must be regarded as a political axiom
that in an equal negotiation agreement will only be reached
if any risks or costs are accepted more or less equally by the
parties. It is not, unfortunately, a military axiom that
reductions can be carried out in such a way as to deny
military advantages equally. Forces can be kept equal or in
the same proportionate balance; but a reduction from one
level of forces to another may open up opportunities to an
aggressor which did not previously exist. This could happen
in a nuclear confrontation, where calculations at the new
levels suggested that the surviving enemy force after a first
strike would not be able to inflict unacceptable damage; or

in a major conventional confrontation, where ground ceased to be saturated and major offensive options opened up; or in a situation such as the Russians must feel exists in East Germany, where reductions below a certain level of forces would make it impossible to maintain control in the event of a West German or N.A.T.O. invasion. Put another way, to ensure (in the McCloy–Zorin phrase) that no states "gain military advantage" may involve more than balance; it may involve abandoning certain kinds of disarmament altogether. The phrase "security is ensured equally for all" is somewhat ambiguous. It might mean (1) that all will have security or (2) that all will have the same amount of security, whether much or little. The first seems the more likely and the more useful objective, though it makes the word "equally" somewhat superfluous. If this is the interpretation, it must be recognized that there can be a conflict between this objective and the need for balanced reductions. The notion that security can be obtained through balanced disarmament needs a great deal more examination than those who drew up the McCloy–Zorin principles have given it; and if it is found that security and balance are in conflict the only possible conclusion is that the McCloy–Zorin principles establish conflicting objectives.

The present Soviet proposal

The Soviet Plan for General and Complete Disarmament must be one of the most drastic proposals ever put to the world by a major power. It sets out in three short stages to abolish all forms of military power, retaining only what are called "police (militia) equipped with light firearms". All general staffs, military budgets and armaments are converted destroyed or abolished "under strict and effective international control". The process is severe and far-reaching and deliberately made so rapid as to leave hesitant governments little time to catch their breath.

The aims of the plan are clearly set out in Article I, which is called Disarmament Obligations. Its wording is as follows:

The states parties to the present treaty solemnly undertake;

1. To carry out, over a period of five years, general and complete disarmament entailing;

The disbanding of all armed forces and the prohibition of their re-establishment in any form whatsoever;

The prohibition and destruction of all stockpiles and the cessation of the production of all kinds of weapons of mass destruction, including atomic, hydrogen, chemical, biological and radiological weapons;

The destruction and cessation of the production of all means of delivering weapons of mass destruction to their targets;

The dismantling of all kinds of foreign military bases and the withdrawal and disbanding of all foreign troops stationed in the territory of any state;

The abolition of any kind of military conscription for citizens;

The cessation of military training of the population and the closing of all military institutions;

The abolition of war ministries, general staffs and their local agencies and all other military and paramilitary establishments and organizations;

The elimination of all types of conventional armaments and military equipment and the cessation of their production, except for the production of strictly limited quantities of agreed types of light firearms for the equipment of the police (militia) contingents to be retained by states after the accomplishment of general and complete disarmament;

The discontinuance of the appropriation of funds for military purposes, whether from state budgets or by organizations or private individuals.

The means by which this would be achieved are obviously subservient to the objective itself. This fact is generally obscured in disarmament negotiations where the objective is taken for granted and debate is about the means. The premise that a disarmed world is bound to be secure is usually common ground: so discussions centre on whether the promised reductions can be adequately inspected or what dangers would emerge in a particular order or timetable. But these questions are secondary. Inspection and verification only become worth analysis once it is established that a particular result is desirable. It is essential, therefore, that any examination of the Soviet Plan should concentrate in the first instance on the basic issue: Is general and complete disarmament down to police (militia) equipped with light firearms desirable? If the answer is affirmative, we must then ask whether this remains true when the limitations of inspection at any particular period are taken into account. Finally, having settled the objectives, the problems of staging and verification can be attacked. The heart of the problem of the Soviet Plan (and also of the American proposals) is not the means of disarmament: it is the end being sought and the extent to which it will increase national security and world security.

Assuming a completely effective system of inspection, the world which would be produced at the end of the third stage of the Soviet Plan would be fundamentally different from the world as it is today. There would be no nuclear weapons whatever and no stockpiles of fissile materials. All military aircraft and rockets would have disappeared; and so would tanks, artillery, heavy army weapons of all kinds, cruisers, destroyers, submarines and so on. All the main means by which nations would conduct hostilities at present would have been destroyed.

On the other hand, weapons for internal security would still exist. Presumably the precise levels of the police (militia) would be determined by the requirements of domestic order. Whether substantially larger forces would be permitted to governments with an internal security problem is not specifically defined, though the treaty would lay down the levels of these forces and establish permitted stockpiles of arms. One assumption in the plan is that these units would be adequate to the fulfilment of the provision of Chapter 7 of the United Nations Charter. They would be made available to the Security Council (under triple command) "for compliance with their obligations in regard to the maintenance of international peace and security under the United Nations Charter". Here is an interesting problem of definition, which would influence the level of forces in the kind of world which the

Russians define as completely disarmed. The Charter provision that forces should be available to the Security Council was not based on the notion that the only troops in existence would be specifically designed for internal security, and that they would be lightly armed and lacking in mobility and such things as air cover. It would almost certainly prove to be true on examination that any effort to fulfil the minimum requirements of Chapter 7 of the Charter would make substantial demands on armed forces above and beyond the elemental needs of domestic order. To impose the will of the world on an organized national state determined to defy it would presumably be a far greater task than, for example, the defeat of a modern insurgency which has only limited resources of wealth and manpower on which to draw. In some terrain, the demands for troops (as in Vietnam, Malaya or Kenya) can be very great.

Theoretically, too, if police (militia) forces were the smallest number necessary for internal security they would place their domestic peace at risk by undertaking an operation on behalf of the Security Council. A world perfectly adapted to the Russian image of general and complete disarmament might therefore be expected to contain substantially more forces than those needed to keep governments secure from their people. Nevertheless, the numbers would be very small compared to the present day; the weapons would be light; and mobility would depend on civil means of transport. The only legitimate international use of force would be an operation mounted on behalf of the Security Council, with the unanimous support of its five permanent members.

There can be little doubt that warfare between states in such a world would be difficult, slow, indecisive and (by twentieth-century standards) relatively harmless. Although this might make war more likely, it could certainly be argued that the choice was worth it. The prospect of political change by long hard battles for local superiority fought by lightly armed troops is not particularly appealing and can certainly not be painted as a utopia. Few whose national memory includes the battles of the Somme have any taste for the conflict of men using rifles and machine guns. But those whose idea of war is associated with Stalingrad or Nagasaki might feel differently. Anyone who knows the effects of thermonuclear weapons and can imagine the circumstances in which they might be used will choose the mud of Flanders at its worst if the choice is offered.

However, this is not the choice. The essential thing about a world made in the Soviet image of general disarmament would be not the armaments that existed but those that might exist. The way to achieve superiority over a rival would not be to launch one's police (militia) against his police (militia) in the hope that it might occupy and dominate his territory; it would be to strain the inspection rules absolutely to the maximum in every important military technology (especially in the production of weapons-grade fissile material) and at a decisive moment to denounce the disarmament agreement and embark on all-out rearmament. For a great power, there would be no sanctions whatever against such an action, since both the Security Council and the peacekeeping forces would be subject to a veto. In any case, the force would not exist to cause any serious damage to a country such as the United States or the Soviet Union. The first country to produce nuclear weapons would then be in a dominant position, especially if these weapons could be used to destroy the nuclear industry of the other side. A denunciation of a treaty of this kind would produce the most unstable arms race conceivable; for the disarmament process would have enfeebled the super-powers while leaving them with all the colossal resources of a modern economy, with a full knowledge of the design and fabrication of weapons of mass destruction, and with experience of modern military thought. Thus, the gap between their actual power, which in strategic terms would be close to nothing, and their potential power would be huge. It is this gap which rearmament or an arms race would be designed to close. The alteration in the levels of power that would result from a rearmament programme in one of the great industrial nations would thus be exceedingly rapid and, if used militarily, decisive.

The fact that actions of this kind could be taken by a rival in a Soviet-type G.C.D. world, would be a central fact in the planning and organization of each of the great powers. Assuming that both sides hoped and believed that the disarmament agreement would be permanently and effectively enforced, they would nevertheless have to keep in mind the prospect of rearmament by dangerous and ambitious rivals. Simple prudence would oblige them to maintain themselves in the best possible situation in the event of a rearmament by the other side. If, one day, the treaty was stretched and then denounced, if there was even a small chance that this would happen, it would be necessary not to fall fatally behind in the ensuing rearmament. Thus, it would be necessary to organize the economy in such a way as to be, in effect, right up against the treaty in every significant respect. As the treaty was being stretched by the other side, one would have to stretch it oneself. The discovery and exploitation of loopholes in the treaty, perhaps through new technological discoveries, could be a major source of power. Governments of important countries could not neglect these possibilities.*

If for some reason a conflict did break out with the kind of forces foreseen in the Soviet proposals, it would not be

* A good example of the response of a great power to a treaty situation in which it must take account of the possibility of abrogation is provided by the testimony of Mr. McNamara on the partial nuclear test ban. He said (Senate hearings, page 107): "Next, I should like to address the problem of surprise abrogation of the treaty. In weighing the military consequences of this treaty, we have naturally considered the risk of sudden Soviet abrogation. The consensus is that the Soviets could not in a single series of tests, however carefully planned those might be, achieve a significant or permanent lead in the strategic field, much less a superweapon capable of neutralizing our deterrent force. Moreover, as long as (1) we maintain the vitality of our weapons laboratories and (2) we retain the administrative and logistic capabilities required to conduct a test series in any environment, the Soviets even with surprise will not be able to achieve a significant time advantage. Therefore, we believe that surprise abrogation does not pose a serious threat to our national security. We will maintain the vitality of our weapons laboratories. We will continue to conduct a programme of underground tests as those may be necessary to meet our military requirements. . . . This ongoing test programme will also include tests designed to lay the foundation for a major atmospheric series to be conducted in case of Soviet abrogation."

settled in infantry encounters by the militia forces. It would be settled in the rearmament race. Fighting with existing forces would be confined to holding operations. Those whose airlines could most quickly be converted to bombers, who had found good economic grounds for building up their fleets of large commercial air transports, whose space programme could be converted quickly to the production of large numbers of accurate rockets with military warheads, would quickly assert their superiority. Because of the overwhelming effect of nuclear weapons, accurately applied, a superiority once achieved could quickly grow to substantial and eventually decisive proportions by being used against the rearmament potential of other great powers.

A Soviet-type G.C.D. would thus have many of the characteristics of a situation of mutual first strike with the interposition of a complex and unpredictable time lag. It is quite possible to argue that no head of government would order a nuclear strike even in a situation in which both sides in a nuclear confrontation are vulnerable to surprise attack; that is, that the great powers are truly defensive in their strategy, that neither really fears the other, that the uncertainties are always too great. But anyone who is sure of this must be entirely content with the present nuclear confrontation. All forms of disarmament, and especially of nuclear disarmament, can be little more than a saving of money to such an optimist. The advocates of G.C.D. can hardly be expected to rely on an argument that even in the worst case the present situation is safe. But their case leads to something very like this: for on examination the pure version of Soviet-type G.C.D. looks remarkably like an exceptionally unstable way of organizing the kind of power which now exists.

It will be argued that while this might be technically true, a situation of general and complete disarmament of this kind would create a new and very different political climate. No man can refute such a claim. All that can be said is that political rivalries have existed at every stage of military technology; and that faced with the existence of operational nuclear weapons in the hands of their enemies, governments (starting with the Imperial Japanese Government in 1945) have shown an unprecedented reluctance to pursue their objectives through the use of force. If there is an argument to be made about creating a new political climate, it is perhaps most defensibly put forward by the advocates of bigger and bigger bombs. The direct and acknowledged influence of American nuclear weapons on the Soviet doctrine of the role of force in international affairs is there for all to see. Those who propose to change political attitudes by altering the number of existing weapons should acknowledge the political effect which the construction of vast destructive power has had in our time; and they must recognize the possibility that disarmament will dissipate the fear of war that modern weapons have created. A Soviet-type G.C.D. system would force even the most trusting power to be ready for instant rearmament; the evidence of others' readiness and the fear of being second would be a major source of tension and it is therefore extraordinarily difficult to see how a better political climate could be expected.

So much for the objective of the Soviet system. It will be recalled that the discussion of it was based on the assumption that whatever inspection was called for under the Treaty was complete and absolutely effective. Thus the situation described in Article 1 (Disarmament Obligations) was assumed to have been fulfilled. In practice, all parties to a treaty would have to take account of the limitations of inspection. The state of inspection and verification technology will determine from time to time what can be done and what cannot be done. Military technology changes constantly, though in a disarmed world it might be expected to change more slowly as a result of a redirection of resources to civil applications. The means by which the possible technologies of the day can be inspected and verified may be expected to develop rapidly as resources and effort are directed into perfecting the control of disarmament. Success in this could extend the limits of what is possible quite extensively over the years. Most of the work now being done on the techniques of inspection is being financed and developed for the purposes of national intelligence agencies;

and undoubtedly the most important disarmament development of recent years is the establishment of satellite photography as the basis of intelligence. If offered enough resources and time, modern technology can be expected to achieve many surprising things. It is unfortunately true that for the present relatively little work is being done anywhere in the world to master the specific technology and techniques of inspection and verification. The partial nuclear test ban of 1962 was held up for some time while the technology of detection was studied and agreed. In the course of examination, the limits of particular kinds of inspection were shown to be very different from what had been expected. It was also learned that the best means of detection of underground tests would be different from what had been anticipated. The demands of a structure for detecting and verifying the conduct of nuclear tests are far less demanding than most kinds of disarmament. Probably the only thing which is comparable is the control of major ship construction. To gain comparable assurance over other major military technologies —armour, airlift capacity for troops, and so on—will demand great experience and resources. New military possibilities will have to be recognized and controlled as they emerge from technical development.

The problem of inspection and verification, then, is inevitably changing. The danger of a reassertion of sovereignty and rearmament, on the other hand, is a permanent and unchanging element in any Soviet-type general disarmament. In general, we can only speculate about whether particular inspection problems will respond to vigorous research and development. In these matters we are judging on present knowledge about methods which have been designed for other purposes (mainly intelligence) and which have worked to different rules in a different climate.

With these qualifications, the most obvious difficulty is secret stocks of nuclear weapons. This disturbing problem has been raised in disarmament speculation, official and academic, for at least ten years. It became common ground between the Soviet Union and the United States in 1955, though the Soviets subsequently put forward plans which ignored what they had previously said. The 1955 formulation (in their plan of 10 May) was as follows:*

The greatest apprehensions exist among peace-loving peoples in connection with the existence of atomic and hydrogen weapons, in regard to which the institution of international control is particularly difficult.

This danger is inherent in the very nature of atomic production. It is well known that the production of atomic energy for peaceful purposes can be used for the accumulation of stocks of explosive atomic materials, and moreover, in ever greater quantities. This means that States having establishments for the production of atomic energy can accumulate, in violation of the relevant agreements, large quantities of explosive materials for the production of atomic weapons. . . .

Thus there are possibilities beyond the reach of international control for evading this control and for organising the clandestine manufacture of atomic and hydrogen weapons, even if there is a formal agreement on international control. In such a situation, the security of the States signatory to the international convention cannot be guaranteed, since the possibility would be open to a potential aggressor to accumulate stocks of atomic and hydrogen weapons for a surprise attack on peace-loving states.

The similar British view was stated succinctly by Mr. Anthony Nutting: "Science simply will not permit us to go forward with an arrangement for eliminating nuclear weapons. It just is not possible; we cannot detect them." Mr. Harold Stassen, for the United States, made the following statement on 20 March 1957:

We also find that when such weapons are fabricated, or when the material is available, either the weapons or the material can be very easily shielded from detection and discovery. One hundred of the most powerful multi-megaton H-bombs can be placed in storage and shielded by relatively simple methods, and then the most sensitive detection apparatus thus far invented by science would give no indication of the presence of this storehouse, even

* Cmd. 9650, pages 613–14, London, H.M.S.O.

if it were brought within 100 yards of its location. A disloyal government could either keep a part of existing stocks or divert without the knowledge of the inspectors, a quantity of fissionable material from which 20, 40, or even 50 multi-megaton bombs could be fabricated. All of this could be carried out without discovery by inspectors, and without the knowledge of other nations, until it was completely accomplished.

Where the present nuclear powers are concerned, the central issue is the fact that a batch of weapons can be taken from the present stockpiles and concealed indefinitely. It is very difficult to imagine how any method of search could ever find them. The best hope would be a system of large rewards which ensured that the secret was known to only a very small number of people—and these would have to trust each other completely over a period extending so far into the future that they would have to be a self-perpetuating group. On the other hand, they would not be the defiant opponents of a world order which they are sometimes painted: they would be much more likely to be a group of loyal government servants detailed to carry out an unpleasant action made necessary by the inevitable assumption that rival powers were doing the same thing.

The only method so far suggested for handling this danger is the detailed tracing of all the records of fissile material production. It is this possibility which explains the emphasis on the possibility of diversion by Mr. Stassen and others. This question has received full and expert examination in the United Kingdom Atomic Energy Authority, which submitted the results of many years of research to the E.N.D.C. on 31 August 1962.*

This paper concluded:

1. A Control Organization could make sure that diversions of current production of plutonium did not exceed 1–2 per cent and on Uranium 235 one per cent.

2. A Control Organization would not be able to guarantee a British figure of past plutonium production to within

* Published as Appendix VI to *Disarm and Verify*, by Sir Michael Wright (London, Chatto and Windus).

10–15 per cent accuracy. If it could be sure that records of electricity supplies to gaseous diffusion plants were accurate, it would not be possible to falsify past U-235 production more than 5–10 per cent; if these records could not be relied on, there might be a margin of 15–20 per cent.

3. In other nuclear powers, it is likely that a control organ would be able to guarantee the number of weapons to within 10–20 per cent varying from country to country.

A substantial nuclear power would probably keep three or four secret stocks, each by an entirely different group of people using a different method. If a country such as the United States maintained four minimum deterrent stocks of 250 weapons each, this would make a total of 1000 out of perhaps 100,000 American weapons, which is 1 per cent. The Soviets could undoubtedly do the same thing without exceeding 3 per cent. Both of these figures are well inside the lower limits set by the British study.

What is the solution to this difficulty? The orthodox western solution (international peace-keeping machinery) will be discussed in the next section. Two attempts by British students of the problem, Mr. Philip Noel-Baker and Mr. Robert Neild, to see through it deserve attention. Mr. Noel-Baker grapples with the problem in his book *The Arms Race,* written in 1959 (London, Stevens). He concedes that "inspection by itself would not provide absolute security either against 'diversion' by a disloyal government of fissile material from new production to warlike use, nor against danger that a government which possesses nuclear weapons might try, in violation of the disarmament treaty, to retain an illicit stock". But he contends that a number of elements, taken together, are sufficient to neutralize this danger. Apart from two which will be considered later (an international nuclear force and the abolition of delivery systems), he sees seven safeguards:

1. A general disarmament agreement would convince the people of the world that governments were resolved to end the arms race and free them from the nuclear menace. "Any government which thereafter broke its pledge by threatening the use of an illicit stock of nuclear weapons,

would have to reckon with the deep hostility of every other nation in the world."

2. The sanctions provided for in the International Atomic Energy Agency statute might be imposed and "may be an important supplementary safeguard against the danger of diversion".

3. A standing commission should be established under the I.A.E.A. to study the control of nuclear disarmament in general and of detecting secret stocks in particular.

4. Possibly (though "the argument is not all on one side") individuals who commit treaty-breaking acts should be personally liable to prosecution and punishment.

5. The Treaty should lay on scientists a personal duty to report a violation of its undertakings.

6. Large rewards should be offered for anyone giving information about a diversion of material or a weapon stock.

7. "The final safeguard against clandestine treaty-breaking diversion of fissile material, and against the retention of secret stocks of nuclear weapons, lies in a drastic reduction of armaments of every kind." He quotes Dr. Oppenheimer in 1953 saying that it will be essential to have a very broad and robust regulation of armaments, in which existing forces and weapons are of a wholly different order than those required for the destruction of one great nation by another, in which steps of evasion will either be too vast to conceal or far too small to have a decisive strategic effect, in view of then existing measures of defence.

These seven arguments and proposals are obviously quite inadequate. The views of world public opinion on anyone using nuclear weapons will be very similar whether they are legitimate or illicit, though the results of the use may be very different; the I.A.E.A. has no conceivable sanction which would bother or even interest the United States or Soviet Union: the I.A.E.A. standing commission would just be the inspectors with another name; people might report to the inspectors, but no nation is going to rely on this possibility for its security against decisive weapons; and the quotation from Dr. Oppenheimer seems to be saying that we must find a way of removing armaments which could be

94

used with decisive strategic effect without suggesting that he knows how this is to be done.

Mr. Neild has argued* that a state cannot threaten with a concealed stock of nuclear weapons because it does not know with any certainty that another state does not also have a concealed stock. The fear of another secret stock is an adequate deterrent to making use of one's own. On this assumption, of course, no major power could take the chance of not having such a stock, since it could be very risky to place reliance on a fear by rivals that you might have weapons which in fact you did not have. A political leader in a potentially enemy country might, for example, become convinced that you are a genuinely honest man; or he might gain intelligence information which proved to his satisfaction that you did not have such a stock. In any case, Mr. Neild's line of argument leads irresistibly to a semi-official recognition of a secret stock in all the nuclear powers, though of unpredictable variety in size and effectiveness. This is not general and complete disarmament: and whatever virtues it may have it cannot be considered to be the proposed Soviet system of G.C.D. Stability based on small nuclear forces on either side would be one thing; a system based on mutual conspiracy of this kind is quite another. It would inevitably introduce important new uncertainties.

The question of a United Nations deterrent to a great power nuclear stock does not arise in the context of the Soviet Plan, where there is (1) no permanent United Nations force, the obligations under Chapter 7 being made up entirely by forces made available by members states when the need arises; and (2) a great power veto over all United Nations action. It will be looked at in connection with the American proposals, where it is the essential element.

Faced with this difficulty and finding no consolation in the sort of arguments which have appealed to Mr. Noel-Baker and Mr. Neild, the Soviet government has taken its stand on quite a different line of defence: the abolition of delivery systems. This position originated with the French Government when it

* "Cheating in a Disarmed World", *Disarmament & Arms Control*, vol. 1, No. 2 (Pergamon Press, 1963).

was embarking on its atomic weapons programme and was particularly anxious to avoid being entangled in arms control agreements which might lead to the control of nuclear facilities, leaving the stockpiles and the delivery systems of the great powers intact. The French therefore suggested that attention should be concentrated on nuclear delivery systems: this would provide a form of disarmament from which France would be excluded for many years. At the same time it offered western support to a means of total nuclear disarmament which did not involve finding a solution to the problem of locating secret stocks. This made an immediate appeal in Moscow.

The Soviet plan now concentrates heavily on destroying all forms of nuclear delivery system. These are abolished in the first stage in a vigorous and exhaustive programme, leaving the nuclear explosives (the bombs and warheads) to be scrapped in the second stage. The destruction of the explosives is tacitly admitted to be unenforceable. We are therefore obliged to ask how effective the abolition of delivery systems will be if it is conceded that a secret stock of thermo-nuclear weapons can relatively easily be concealed and maintained by the large powers, and that it is virtually certain to be.

At present, the main means of nuclear delivery in the United States, the Soviet Union, Britain and France are ballistic missiles in submarines, in land-based silos, and mobile on land; light, medium and heavy bombers; army bombardment missiles of various ranges; depth charges, land mines, and a variety of small tactical weapons, including artillery and mortars. It is perhaps possible to contemplate concealing a small number of certain of these weapons for a period. But those with any substantial range are so complex and in need of such constant maintenance and replacement of parts that it is unlikely that they could be relied on for more than a few years in a secret place. Established military means of delivery can therefore probably be effectively eliminated, given broad powers and a substantial period of years; and with adequate control new production would be difficult. On the other hand, the disappearance of all armaments except light infantry drastically lowers the requirements for effectiveness in weapons.

Improvisation, which has always played an important part in war, would be given an unusual importance when it was recognized that states possessed thermonuclear bombs of devastating power and had only the problem of getting them to a target. The obvious solution is to use the aircraft of the day. Both airliners and freighters seem likely to exist in increasing numbers, carrying increasing loads at high speeds and altitudes. It was stated by a British delegate to the Geneva negotiations that a thermonuclear weapon now exists which has a length of five feet and a diameter of two feet: and that was before the age of multiple warheads, with their obviously striking reduction in volume and weight. If there is any doubt that several thermonuclear explosives could be carried by modern airlines, one need only note that they already make provision under their wing to carry a spare engine. The main requirement in converting a modern airliner into a bomber would be a release mechanism and (if existing safety standards are to be observed) an electrical control system which would permit the crew to arm the weapon at the desired moment. Self-contained navigation systems are now in general use in airliners. Indeed, the Doppler system now widely used was designed originally for strategic bombers.

What an inspection system might ensure is that airliners were not ready for immediate conversion to use as nuclear delivery systems. But the production of the necessary associated equipment would be easy to conceal and the job of converting the airliners would take only a very short time —probably no more than a few days, if that. The difficult technical problem of nuclear explosives is solved by the secret stock; and the massive industrial achievement of a vehicle which will fly many thousands of miles to a precise position carrying heavy weight is unfortunately solved at great expense for the benefit of the travelling public. It must therefore be recognized that in the conditions of general disarmament visualized by the Soviet Union massive counter-city attacks with thermonuclear weapons would remain within the power of the United States, the Soviet Union, the United Kingdom, France and possibly others, provided they were prepared to evade the provisions of the treaty in certain essential respects. It can be argued that this situation would retain a certain elemental stability, though certainly nothing like the stability of the present confrontation; what cannot be argued is that this can be called either general and complete disarmament or nuclear disarmament.

Apart from the question of nuclear weapons, the Soviet plan inevitably dismantles much of what is now regarded by many nations, including the Soviet Union itself, as the security system. The immediate abolition of all foreign bases, for example, would drastically change the character of Europe, and especially of Germany. It is hard to imagine that the Soviet Union really believes that it would be sensible and profitable to enter into an agreement under which all Soviet forces were withdrawn from East Germany and Poland. It is true that at the same time the great object of inducing the United States to withdraw all her forces from Europe would be achieved: but this transfer of the destiny of western Europe back to its people is scarcely designed to appeal to any of the Potsdam powers—least of all the Soviet Union.

Nevertheless, it is possible to argue that the Soviet Plan would be in the long-term interests of the Soviet Union as understood by the Soviet Government. Nuclear disarmament would reduce the Americans to equality with the Soviets through secret stocks. It would remove the qualitative superiority of American delivery systems. Any danger there might be that the Soviet Union might once again be invaded by its enemies would clearly be removed. While the Soviet armed forces would obviously become very weak, general disarmament would make the defensive strength of large populations decisive. The orthodox Communist view (now more commonly held in Peking than in Moscow) is that chaos in the underdeveloped world, with the capitalist powers removed, would help the cause of world Communism. The strength of governments would be reduced and the task of subversion made easier. Where the Soviet Union itself was concerned, the expenditure of perhaps 18 per cent of the gross national product on defence could be avoided and these massive resources devoted to the development of the economy. If in the course of time the country reached a level of economic strength where it felt its influence would be increased by asserting itself as a major power, the old rules of sovereignty could always be re-established by a simple denunciation of the treaty and a return to self-sufficient power as the source of security. These considerations suggest that while the Soviet Government obviously does not expect its plan to be accepted it would not be thrown into total confusion if it were. The Russians probably feel they have much less to lose than their western rivals, whose great network of trade, alliances and influence throughout the continents would take on a new character if something close to anarchy was settled on the world by international agreement.

The U.S. proposals

On 18 April 1962 the United States Government submitted its "Outline of Basic Provisions of a Treaty on General and Complete Disarmament in a Peaceful World". For many years this has formed (with the Russian Plan) the basis for the Geneva negotiations on general and complete disarmament. These proposals are generally assumed to represent a position which the United States would regard as highly desirable and from which, within certain limits, the U.S. Government would be prepared to move in a negotiation. The other three N.A.T.O. powers in the Geneva negotiations (Britain, Italy and Canada) have given full support to the U.S. position. Generally speaking, the neutrals have been concerned to reconcile the Soviet and American stands; and in the absence of other comprehensive schemes it might be assumed that the entire range of world opinion represented in Geneva (excluding, that is, France, China and their clients) supports either the American or the Soviet approach. In any real terms, however, this would be very presumptuous. It is possible to argue that the Soviet Plan might be genuinely intended by the Soviet Government because of the advantages which could be conferred by equality and the abolition of extra-national power to the point of anarchy. No such claim can be made for the American approach to the American proposals. They aim at a peaceful world where power will be the agent of law; they recognize the problem of power in the disarmed world; they try to lay down general principles for dealing with it; and it is impossible to avoid the conclusion that they fail. The great central problem of the disarmament process—who is to possess decisive physical power? —is in the end avoided.

The American proposals provide for three stages designed to achieve certain defined objectives according to stated principles. The objectives are to ensure that disarmament is general and complete and that war is no longer used to settle international problems; and at the same time it is planned to establish reliable procedures for settling disputes and effective arrangements for maintaining the peace. To these ends, armed forces would be disbanded, armament production would cease, stocks of weapons would be destroyed, military training would end, and military expenditure would be discontinued. Forces remaining to states would be those which were necessary for internal security (and would not include nuclear weapons). A United Nations Peace Force would be "equipped with agreed types of armaments necessary to ensure that the United Nations can effectively deter or suppress any threat or use of arms". An International Disarmament Organization would have "unrestricted access to all places as necessary for the purpose of effective verification". The principles on which this would be done are effectively those of the McCloy–Zorin statement with the additional American requirement that verification would be designed to ensure that throughout the disarmament process agreed levels of armaments and forces were not exceeded.

The first stage would take three years from the entry into force of the treaty. In each of these years, the parties to the treaty would destroy 10 per cent of their existing stocks of the main armaments, having declared the quantities of the main types which they possess. Over the three years, American and Russian armed forces would be reduced to 2·1 million and, generally speaking, others would be restricted to 1 per cent of population or 100,000, whichever was higher. The production of fissionable material for nuclear weapons would stop and an agreed quantity of weapons-grade Uranium 235 would be transferred from existing stocks to non-weapons purposes. Fissile material would not be transferred between states for weapons; nuclear weapons themselves would not be transferred and non-nuclear powers would not manufacture them; nuclear tests would be abolished; and weapons of mass destruction would not be put into outer space. The International Disarmament Organization would be established with a general conference of all parties to the treaty, a control council with permanent and rotating members, and an Administrator. A subsidiary body called the International Commission on Reduction of the Risks of War would be established to make recommendations about how the risk of war by accident, miscalculation, failure of communications or surprise attack might be reduced during the disarmament process. The parties to the treaty would also support the establishment of a United Nations Peace Observation Corps which would have a standing group of observers to investigate situations which constituted a threat to peace.

The second stage would follow, subject to Stage I being carried out satisfactorily and the accession to the treaty of all militarily significant states. During its three years, one half of the remaining major armaments which had been reduced 30 per cent in Stage I would be abolished. The disarmament of smaller weapons not included in Stage I would also begin. One-half of existing stockpiles of chemical and biological weapons would be abolished. One-half of the remaining armed forces of the United States and Soviet Union would be abolished and the agreed levels for other states would in no case exceed the American–Russian total. The amounts of fissionable materials to be permitted to states would be agreed and reduction to this level would be carried out by removing these materials and transferring them to non-weapons purposes and by destroying the non-nuclear components of these weapons. Agreed military bases would be dismantled. All parties to the treaty would accept the compulsory jurisdiction of the International Court of Justice. The subsidiary body of the International Disarmament Organization which was working on the rules of international conduct would recommend rules to the Control Council. If these were accepted, they would become effective unless a majority of the parties to the treaty disapproved. Individual parties to the treaty could notify the I.D.O. within a year that they did not consider themselves bound by these rules. The United Nations Peace Force would be established.

In the third stage, all armaments remaining would be eliminated except those agreed to be necessary for internal order and to protect the personal security of citizens. Armed forces would be reduced to the levels needed for internal security and for the provision of "agreed manpower for the United Nations Peace Force". The parties to the treaty would eliminate all nuclear weapons remaining at their disposal and would dismantle or convert to peaceful uses all facilities for their production. "The parties to the treaty would progressively strengthen the United Nations Peace Force established in Stage II until it had sufficient armed forces and armaments so that no state could challenge it."

This plan is a very substantial piece of work, and extensive supporting analysis has been done by many people, especially in the United States. However, almost all of the proposals and virtually all of the work done on them are devoted to the means by which the disarmament process is achieved. The basic questions go unasked. The entire definition of the security system which the world is to have at the end of the third stage is contained in the following paragraphs.

I. Objectives are defined as follows:

1. To ensure that (a) disarmament is general and complete and war is no longer an instrument for settling international problems, and (b) general and complete disarmament is accompanied by the establishment of reliable procedures for the settle-

ment of disputes and by effective arrangements for the maintenance of peace in accordance with the principles of the Charter of the United Nations.

Paragraph II of the Objectives abolishes all armed forces, weapons and military expenditure subject to two remaining requirements:

III. To ensure that, at the completion of the program for general and complete disarmament, states would have at their disposal only those non-nuclear armaments, forces, facilities and establishments as are agreed to be necessary to maintain internal order and protect the personal security of citizens.

IV. To ensure that during and after implementation of general and complete disarmament, states also would support and provide agreed manpower for a United Nations Peace Force to be equipped with agreed types of armaments necessary to ensure that the United Nations can effectively deter or suppress any threat or any use of arms.

2. Under "Principles", the same general point is made:

4. As national armaments are reduced, the United Nations would be progressively strengthened in order to improve its capacity to ensure international security and the peaceful settlement of differences as well as to facilitate the development of international co-operation in common tasks for the benefit of mankind.

3. Nothing would be done to create an international force in the first stage. However, the following section is included in the Stage I proposals under the heading "Measures to Strengthen Arrangements for Keeping the Peace":

5. United Nations Peace Force.
The parties to the treaty would undertake to develop arrangements during Stage I for the establishment in Stage II of a United Nations Peace Force. To this end, the parties to the treaty would agree on the following measures within the United Nations:

(a) Examination of the experience of the United Nations leading to a further strengthening of United Nations forces for keeping the peace;

(b) Examination of the feasibility of concluding promptly the agreements envisaged in Article 43 of the United Nations Charter;

(c) Conclusion of an agreement for the establishment of a United Nations Peace Force in Stage II, including definitions of its purpose, mission, composition and strength disposition, command and control, training, logistical support, financing, equipment and armaments.

In Stage II, under "Measures to Strengthen Arrangements for Keeping the Peace", the following is proposed:

3. United Nations Peace Force.

The United Nations Peace Force to be established as the result of the agreement reached during Stage I would come into being within the first year of Stage II and would be progressively strengthened during Stage II.

Stage III also has a section on "Measures to Strengthen Arrangements for Keeping the Peace":

3. United Nations Peace Force.

The parties to the treaty would progressively strengthen the United Nations Peace Force established in Stage II until it had sufficient armed forces and armaments so that no state could challenge it.

That is all the definition which is offered. Though the means are left open, the objective is clear: international armed forces will be of such a strength and character that no state will be able to challenge them. But issues which can only be regarded as essential to any consideration of what the U.S. proposals really mean are covered by formulas about these matters being for future discussion.

A semi-official (even if non-American) interpretation of the American proposals has been given by Sir Michael Wright, who as leader of the British delegation to the Geneva Disarmament Conferences from 1959 to 1963 had the duty of defending this approach to general and complete disarmament. He writes:*

* *Disarm and Verify*, op. cit., pp. 89-91.

They (the United States proposals) specify a U.N. peace force to be equipped with agreed types of arms necessary to ensure that the United Nations can effectively deter or suppress any threat or use of arms; that arrangements should be made in Stage I for the establishment of the peace force in Stage II, and that it be progressively strengthened during Stages II and III until it had sufficient armed forces and armaments so that no state could challenge it. The United States plan does not stipulate where the contingents are to be stationed or how they should be composed; it does not contemplate a *troika* command. It points to the Security Council as the body which would decide upon the use of the force but specifically provides for an agreement to be concluded in Stage II upon all problems concerning the force, including command and control. In other words, it does not provide for a veto within the High Command on action by the force; and it leaves the question of a veto in the Security Council by a permanent Member on the use of the force as a matter for further consideration and negotiation. . . .

It (the American plan) contemplates a peace-keeping force international in structure, with integrated and veto-free command, and if necessary possessing, at least for the time being, nuclear weapons which would enable it to deal with any potential violator or aggressor. Where it is less specific is over the question of the international body which would finance, equip and direct the force. It refrains from pronouncing definitely one way or the other on the question whether this body should be the Security Council of the United Nations as at present constituted, that is to say a body of twelve members* of which the five permanent members possess a veto upon action under Chapter VII of the Charter.

Sir Michael suggests three possible alternatives:†

1. Some new body which is not provided for in the U.N. Charter and which will by-pass the Security Council in dealing with threats to the peace, as defined in Chapter VII of the Charter.

2. To amend the Charter so that in this context (the power to

* This was written before the enlargement of the Security Council.
† Op. cit., p. 91.

use and direct a peace-keeping force in a disarmed world) the Security Council could take a decision by a two-thirds or conceivably a majority vote, without the power of veto for any state.

3. To place the responsibility upon the U.N. Assembly, perhaps by a two-thirds vote.

Sir Michael says it would be out of place to seek to push this analysis further in the present context. "The essential point of note is that the United States and the United Kingdom have shown themselves willing to explore the various possibilities involved, while the Soviet Union has so far set its face rigidly against any amendment of the Charter, or any by-passing of the Charter which would involve the abolition or the weakening of the Soviet power of veto. Yet without agreement on precisely this, the whole concept of general and complete disarmament carried out in three consecutive and uninterrupted stages is most unlikely to be realized, and it is misleading to pretend otherwise."

The same doctrine at an earlier stage of evolution can be seen in the British position, as outlined by Mr. Selwyn Lloyd in a 1959 speech to the United Nations, which preceded Mr. Khrushchev's proclamation of the same doctrine by a day. Mr. Lloyd proposed three stages, in the first of which "we should study the nature and functions of the international control organ which will not only have to control disarmament measures, but also will have increasing responsibilities within the framework of the United Nations to preserve world peace as purely national armaments diminish".* In the third, "the international control organ should reach its final form and attain its full capability for keeping peace".

It is clear from all these quotations that the great problem of power in the disarmed world has been a continuing theme in the Anglo-American approach to disarmament. The unquestioned image has been one of a "peace-keeping

* In later western thinking, as represented by the 1962 U.S. proposals, the inspection and verification organization, called the International Disarmament Organization, became divorced from the peace-keeping body, called the United Nations Peace Force.

force", capable of exercising a predominant force in the world. The central phrase is no doubt that used in the American third-stage proposal—"so that no state could challenge it". But there is also the formulation in the section on Objectives that a U.N. Peace Force should be able "to ensure that the United Nations can effectively deter or suppress any threat or any use of arms".

In spite of the voluminous American literature on arms control, analysis of the totally disarmed world has received little attention. Professor Lincoln P. Bloomfield has undertaken it* and concluded that the United States proposals carry the unmistakable meaning of world government with enough power to keep the peace and enforce its judgements. He considers that such a system is probably unattainable without disarmament. But in order to avoid creating a situation "which would almost surely bring on a war" through disarmament, the crucial thing is the provision of an effective international force. He believed that this would need about half a million men and a nuclear force adequate to deter any likely clandestine violation of the disarmament agreement. (This level of force might be compared in general terms to the present British armed forces.) Having laid down his minimum requirements, including some form of legislative system, he concludes that "at present the very notion of a politico-military rubric superior to both East and West seems remote". As with many other American writers, he foresees an adoption of world government only in the event of a drastic reduction in the present levels of world security.

The implications of a U.N. force that can conduct decisive actions—whether in support of decisions of the International Court (whose compulsory jurisdiction all would accept) or to head off a threat to the peace—are still in need of full analysis. Even Professor Bloomfield's highly sceptical analysis seems to underrate the scope of a security system based on such a force. It is not enough to be able to act by

* In 1962 in "A World Effectively Controlled by the United Nations", Study Memorandum No. 7, prepared for the Institute for Defence Analyses, 1710 H Street N.W., Washington 6.

majority decision of the Security Council, for this provides no remedy against actions by an effective majority against the security interests of the minority. This would in present circumstances provide the Soviet Union and its allies, for example, with no effective machinery for enforcing their security interests. France and China would feel the same way, and the day may come when the United States may find herself in this position.* Effective political machinery would have to be able to take decisions independent of even a substantial majority of powers. There would have to be a higher direction of the forces which would take the necessary military measures, even in the event of hostility to the action by many states; and there would have to be enough force to impose the will of the International Court or the central executive authorities on the greatest power, or combination of powers, in the world. The need to deal with the United States and Soviet Union simultaneously can perhaps be dismissed. What is certain, however, is that the U.N. Peace Force would have to be able to handle the situation if either decided to break the treaty at important points. It would also have to be able to deter unequivocally a great-power decision to rearm—even in the event of a strong coalition (such as the United States now leads) supporting the offending power. Such a United Nations Peace Force would have to be able to impose its physical control over a United States of America which possessed a substantial secret stock of nuclear weapons, was supported by western Europe, Japan and some Western Hemisphere governments, and which had embarked on a series of actions which the Soviet Union alleged, and the International Court agreed,† were

* "Would the United States itself (Professor Bloomfield asks) seriously consider disbanding its own armaments and abrogating to an international authority beyond its direct control the authority and the power to do those things which in modern history have been the prerogative of the nation?"

† The usefulness of the International Court for this purpose may be doubted. It would probably take 9–12 months to make its judicial finding; and under its present Statute the Court is not intended to act as a fact-finding Commission but to pronounce on points of law. But

designed to give it military dominance. A peace-keeping operation of this kind—it is perhaps easier for western minds to imagine it in relation to the Soviet Union—could be little less than a world war. Even a disarmed United States or Soviet Union would have a massive capacity to resist invasion. In fact, the forces which in the end would carry the brunt of the peace-keeping action would almost certainly have to be drawn from the rival of the offending power after an appropriate (and no doubt mutual) rearmament.

It is all but impossible to conceive of this kind of force being at the command of central world institutions. If things did develop to this point, however, the resulting executive and high command could be described only as a world government. Whether this is technically possible is an open question; but there must be the most serious doubt about whether any of the permanent members of the Security Council can conceive of a political body close to the present institutions which they would be prepared to accept as dominant over them in military terms.* A balance of forces in the United Nations, and especially in the Security Council, which is acceptable to the United States will not be acceptable to the Soviet Union. It is probable that no foreseeable balance of forces will be acceptable to either.

* Mr. Harold Macmillan, when British Minister of Defence, appeared to be thinking along these lines. He told the House of Commons in 1955 that disarmament must include all weapons. "Control must provide effective international or, if we like, supranational authority invested with real power. Hon. members may say that this is elevating the United Nations, or whatever may be the authority, into something like world government. Be it so. It is none the worse for that. In the long run, this is the only way out for mankind." (*House of Commons Debates*, 2 March 1955, col. 2815.)

Mr. Duncan Sandys said much the same thing in the British Defence White Paper of 1958: "The ultimate aim must be comprehensive disarmament by all nations, coupled with comprehensive inspection and control by a world authority. Nothing less than this makes sense." (London, H.M.S.O. Cmnd. 363.)

clearly the Western powers intend that the Court should be adapted or some new body created which would command the confidence of all nations.

In any case, there is no real escape from the fact that the only answer to clandestine Soviet rearmament would be American rearmament, and vice versa; and that the only answer to an assertion of Soviet sovereignty would be an assertion of American sovereignty, and vice versa. The possibility that this would happen would continue until the whole political character of the disarmed world had changed fundamentally. Another generation could deal with this situation when it arose according to its own outlook and standards. For our time, the basis of a disarmed or reorganized world must be a recognition that this can always happen and that there is no realistic way to legislate against it. The problem is to ensure that a return to a purely sovereign world will hold no temptations for any powers and so will not be feared by others. The central problem in the present context is clearly the U.S.–Soviet rivalry. Should the treaty be denounced, it is essential that the resulting confrontation should be one which everyone can see to be stable. In these circumstances, there should be no temptation to denounce the treaty and (even more important) no fear that the other side might be tempted to denounce it. To be stable and acceptable, a disarmament treaty must rest on the belief that if it was swept away with all its machinery there would still be security. The only alternative to an underlying stability of this kind is a political structure clearly able to decide to act against a great power and a military establishment able and willing to follow this up with effective force. These conditions are obviously too demanding for the United States, the Soviet Union, Britain, France, China and many others, even if the military requirements can be met; and there is no reason to think that the first step towards disarmament will alter this fact. If this is accepted, the objectives of the American proposals disappear into unreality. The American image of the disarmed world is as little able to handle its central problem (though more able to handle lesser peace-keeping problems) as the Soviet image of a disarmed world. It too would be tense, uncertain and insecure.

In one form or another, this line of argument has been widely conceded in official Western circles. It is recognized that general disarmament of the kind foreseen in the U.S. proposals of 1962 is a long way off and belongs to a very different political climate. It is pointed out that there is no time limit for the third stage; and there is no disposition to discuss what the time limit might be. The Soviet Plan is one which the Powers are invited to negotiate and agree and then proceed to carry out, subject only to the assurance that it has been carried out faithfully and honestly and that the control system is functioning effectively. The Soviet Government argues that it is ready now to embark on total disarmament down to the levels it proposes. Although the American third stage might suggest that this is the case with their plan as well, the absence of a time limit introduces a fundamental distinction. The third stage is not something which is now on the table in any real way; it is a direction in which it is hoped that the world will evolve when the cooling balm of the first two stages has (in the familiar imagery) banished tension, eased the arms race and restored the faith and hope of mankind. Just how much American thinking is attached to the arrival of some political New Jerusalem was shown in a remarkable statement of the acting head of the U.S. delegation to the Geneva Conference, Mr. James F. Leonard, when the Italians made their inconvenient effort in 1970 to re-launch G.C.D. Mr. Leonard had said* that progress towards G.C.D. could only accompany concrete progress towards a more peaceful world. He then said what he meant by this: "Such a peaceful world, in which general and complete disarmament could be realized, would be a world in which the rule of law, and not the use of force, prevailed in relations between states; a world in which there were agreed standards of international behaviour; a world in which effective means of enforcing international agreements and settling disputes had been established and were utilized; a world in which there prevailed a spirit of confidence, openness and a recognized community of interests among states.'† Making all allowances for the forms of rhetoric

* See above, page 75.

† Official report, Continuing Committee on Disarmament, Geneva, 23 June 1970.

which are traditional to American politics, it can be said as a minimum that only those who believe there are independent forces working for the perfectability of international society can acknowledge the American proposals as serious on their own definitions; and for most people they can be said to be linked to conditions which on any reading of history or analysis of reality cannot be anticipated.

But is it not desirable, many will ask, to have so amiable an objective against the possibility of dramatically happier days? Even this modest line of argument offers many difficulties. In the first place, there are unavoidable consequences in keeping the idea of the disarmed world as the distant objective. Arms reductions are advocated and are by implication desirable because they serve the long term interest, even if they may be undesirable in themselves. It is possible that risks may be taken in earlier stages to achieve an objective of complete disarmament which is not, in fact, an objective at all. Military stability could conceivably be placed at risk with a resulting increase, rather than decrease, in tension. A more certainly predictable result— one, indeed, which can already be seen—is that many who conscientiously believe general disarmament would undermine security will oppose lesser disarmament or arms controls agreements that are in themselves desirable. Measures that demonstrably increase security will be suspected if they are proposed as first steps towards the insecure world of the U.S. third stage. It is possible that many in the United States Senate, and also in the Defense Department, oppose first- and second-stage measures precisely because they believe that they are designed to lead to the third stage. At the same time, serious long-term dangers (such as destabilizing technological developments or the spread of nuclear weapons) are allowed to develop because it is felt that in some vague way "disarmament" or "world government" will save the day in the end.

Politicians are saved from despair by the sense that amid the jargon of the Geneva negotiations (if they can be called negotiations) there is a plan that with a better political atmosphere and a few compromises can be put into effect.

The professional servants of governments in the security field—senior officers, defence civilians and scientists, diplomats who have specialized in political and military subjects—seldom share this view. Politicians and the public they represent are entitled to hope; but at present their hopes are attached to a scheme which offers no way out and which cannot claim to be even a long-term plan for reform. When the top is lifted from the western proposals, there is nothing there but faith in the self-perpetuation of the present system of power.

This chapter has taken general and complete disarmament seriously as a security system because of the great place it occupies in the public posture of the *status quo* powers. While privately they may be sceptical about G.C.D. there is no evidence that they have other broad directions for reform to suggest beyond the promotion of better relations and moderation leading to certain measures of arms control. Under the broad definition of collateral measures to G.C.D., many valuable and relevant measures for improving international security have been proposed by the various participants in the Geneva disarmament conferences and elsewhere. These have been placed in the broad context of G.C.D. which, it is claimed, will be made easier by their application: but in reality they are plans designed either to improve international security generally or to add to the security of those proposing them. Many are realistic and of general advantage: and some of considerable significance have been adopted. Yet they are nominally relegated to some distant G.C.D. objective in a context expressed by a British Government statement of 1968:*

The ultimate goal of United Kingdom policy is an agreement for general and complete disarmament. But we recognize that such a far-reaching objective will not be quickly or easily achieved and that long and patient negotiations lie ahead. At present, therefore, we think it wise to work for international agreement on

* *Disarmament: The Path to Peace*, prepared by the Foreign Office and issued by Her Majesty's Government, April 1968 (London, H.M.S.O.), paragraph 19.

more limited measures of arms control (sometimes called collateral or partial measures) which we think are urgently needed and
which we believe are attainable. The arms control measures on
which attention has been mainly focused are a treaty to prevent
the spread of nuclear weapons and a comprehensive nuclear test
ban. Measures of this sort, if they can be achieved, will constitute important steps towards a safer and saner world. They
would improve the international atmosphere, reduce tension and
build up confidence. They would thus prepare the way for further
measures, leading eventually to the final goal.

This statement expresses perfectly, and typically, the
false linkage between G.C.D. and whatever active negotiations there may be for arms control. The official view of the
main western governments is that G.C.D. is a harmless
objective which creates a constant incentive to go further
and do better. It is a sort of ideal condition against which a
fallen but struggling world order can measure its achievements.

Serious attention to this objective, however, suggests that
it would by no means produce an ideal condition: and in
simple tactical terms there must be the most serious doubts
about whether its maintenance as a nominal goal is as
innocent as is believed. The longer-term image is immensely
important for what is being done in the short term. If an
international security order is being slowly built to withstand
the shocks to which technology, proliferation, ignorant men,
new issues and disintegrating states will inevitably expose it,
its ultimate shape is very important. Clearly, a detailed
design is impossible. But if we cannot see any shape at all
in the thing we are actually building and imagine that it is
really a disarmed world, we may make some critical errors.

As a preliminary to making any real progress towards a
new organization of power, the objective of general and
complete disarmament should therefore be dropped. Those
familiar with American policy will say that this has already
happened, that the absence of a time limit on Stage III of the
U.S. proposals puts it effectively beyond policy. But until
G.C.D. is dropped from the public stance represented by the

1968 British Government position (above), it will be an important hindrance to the real reform of power.

No one can know with any certainty how important advocacy of G.C.D. is to the world influence and position of the United States, the Soviet Union, Britain and others who have taken it up. The way in which the Geneva G.C.D. meetings are ignored by the world public can give little consolation to those who persuaded their governments that only by taking up G.C.D. could they make an important impact on what is called world public opinion. There must be some significance in the fact that the debates on G.C.D. dragged on for years without being reported or noticed and were then put on one side in favour of "collateral measures". Disarmament as at present advocated by the great powers has remarkably little appeal to anyone, unless the news media are all miscalculating. The reason for this is probably that people have a fairly reliable capacity to distinguish between the serious and the propagandist and cannot be deceived for long.

Although it would clearly be a difficult feat for a leading government competing for world influence to break openly with G.C.D., it is possible that, properly handled, this could be a source of influence. A reputation for integrity and seriousness can be an important asset in international affairs. At any rate, this issue must be settled by governments having weighed carefully the risks that a break with G.C.D. would involve. Conversely, before deciding that they must go on proclaiming their faith in something they rightly and conscientiously know to be dangerous, they should recognize that there are at least six major advantages to be gained from a formal recantation:

1. It would remove the notion that all serious measures of disarmament or arms control are first steps towards complete disarmament. This reputation makes them very much less acceptable to those who are concerned for security. The chiefs of staff of the important countries and some legislators may welcome a nuclear test ban for itself but suspect it to the extent that it eases the way towards general disarmament. Thus, holding to an objective that undermines security

exposes any attempt to build a more secure world order to the opposition of the powerful elements in any government which are professionally concerned with security. The professional military advisers of governments have enormous power because they accept responsibility for the security of the state. It seems extraordinary to invite their opposition in order to achieve a public relations image of doubtful value.

2. It would allow preliminary measures of arms control or disarmament to be judged in relation to seriously held objectives. In the present context, all measures abolishing arms are alleged to serve the cause of peace and security, and all increases or alterations are assumed to be hostile to these objects. This may not be true. If the objective is in fact something very different from the Russian or American third stages, different first steps may be required to achieve it. While the objective of G.C.D. remains on the table, there is a natural prejudice against measures which might, for example, secure a condition of mutual invulnerability and in favour of measures which reduce force levels or inhibit innovation. First stages of the type of the American plan concern themselves with such things as 30 per cent reductions in wide ranges of armaments which may make very little sense if they are not part of a scheme for general disarmament.

3. It is often contended that mankind needs the hope of a disarmed world to sustain it under the shadow of nuclear destruction. As long as this hope is based on proposals which lack seriousness, it may be doubted whether it is very widely or genuinely felt. Far greater satisfaction seems to have been derived from the partial ban on nuclear tests than from the G.C.D. proposals, which outside the Warsaw Pact countries have attracted little attention. The reason for this is surely that the partial ban was actually negotiated and signed and atmospheric tests by the signatory powers ceased. Hopes permanently attached to unreality must eventually lead to cynicism or even to a climate of opinion which may drive weak governments to do things which undermine security.

4. In many countries great moral energy is directed towards finding a safe and peaceful world. Much of this effort is now working for some form of general disarmament. There

are signs that the more extreme advocates of an indefinite extension of the present system welcome the absorption of the idealists in such a vain pursuit. They can argue that this gives the conscientious a noble vision and the believers in national military force an assurance that they will not be impeded by international arrangements. Such a situation can satisfy none but the more simple-minded believers in the sovereign state system as it now exists. The organization of the world is not so safe and so desirable that radical moral energies are best diverted towards unreal objectives. Quite the contrary. The achievement of a new unity between realism and idealism could be of inestimable benefit.

5. The failure to achieve G.C.D., or to make any significant progress towards it, is taken as a sign that international relations are still at too primitive a stage to contemplate a joint reform of the power system. This could conceal the fact that the political winds are as favourable now as they are ever likely to be.

6. Perhaps the most serious objection to maintaining G.C.D. as the final aim is that governments are unlikely to put a major effort into forming an international security system while they still cling to an undefined hope that in better days (or, indeed, if things get worse) there is the prospect of general disarmament. The lingering sense that G.C.D. is the ultimate solution makes it difficult to begin on a long and arduous task which will undoubtedly require governments to make decisions demanding persistence, courage and expense.

THE MACHINERY OF REFORM

PROPOSALS and agreements about security have occupied a special place in the political thought and practice of most countries throughout this century. Whatever their views about the desirability of limiting in some way their national freedom of action in security affairs, most governments are conscious of public disquiet about the dangers of war and the economic and political costs of armed forces. Much influential opinion is believed to be anxious to achieve radical reductions in troops and expenditures. These assumptions vary from country to country and from time to time. The most pacific countries—India after 1962 for example—are capable of a powerful surge of opinion in favour of more troops, more arms and a more determined use of military power: and this has been accompanied by a remarkable hardening of feeling towards arms control and disarmament proposals. All attitudes are clearly subject to change in the light of national experience. Nevertheless, one can say that for a long time it has been evident in countries like Britain, Mexico, Brazil, Canada, Sweden or Norway that no politician would allow himself to become publicly identified with scepticism about disarmament agreements. In the United States and the Soviet Union, those in power are careful to appear to be generally favourable to disarmament, at least under the right circumstances. At the same time, however, orthodox military opinion has been and remains dubious about the value of international arms control arrangements of any kind: and this scepticism is fed by the feeling that those who favour disarmament are unconcerned with the problems of security, or are prone to optimistic assumptions.

This confused climate gives an unprofessional character to all debates about the reform of power through disarmament and arms control. The higher morality traditionally surrounding the subject makes people reluctant to recognize that disarmament proposals, concessions, withdrawals, propaganda and agreements all play a part in the political game, both domestic and international. Any new security order will have to make sense in this context and will only be agreed and sustained if it can exploit these political forces.

The main literature of arms control is concentrated on the problems of security to the neglect of the more purely political issues. The idea of agreed management of some aspects of armaments is in a real sense a branch of military studies; and those who advocate it are seeking through international arrangements to achieve what can only be described as military or security objectives. But as with all security objectives the means must be political. All arms control and disarmament negotiations are related to power, and power is in most cases the heart of the political process. The social and ideological traditions that surround the military forces of most countries (and are reflected in the anti-militarist and internationalist traditions of the left) also help to guarantee that arms control or disarmament negotiations will be highly political.

Negotiations of this kind must take place between governments and governments always have political objectives. Unless they perceive an urgent security need, they will give precedence to these objectives, which can be either foreign or domestic. New departures in international security are therefore possible only if the right politicians in the right places decide that they are in their interest. International security arrangements such as the ban on the use of chemical weapons, on nuclear testing in the atmosphere, or on the proliferation of nuclear weapons have been reached at a certain time by certain powers. Some countries adhere to them and others reject them. Everyone is aware of their bearing on the security of particular countries. At the time they were negotiated, some politicians had a domestic interest in achieving them and others had a domestic sentiment which was opposed to them. A particular order existed when they were adopted, with certain powers able to persuade others to go along with them. But this world order changes steadily, with the rise and decline of particular powers and the strengthening and weakening of international links of various kinds. Military technology also changes, and this alters the importance of any particular agreement. New foreign policies, new alliances, new men come on to the scene. International organizations gain the loyalty of some and the hostility of others depending on how they conduct themselves. Sometimes quickly, sometimes slowly, the international order groups and regroups with the changing fears and hopes of those who make it. Unexpected events—a Cuban missile crisis, a Suez intervention, a Congo disintegration, the technical possibility of a reasonably effective missile defence system, an accessible method of uranium enrichment, the opening of the sea bed or outer space to exploitation—make governments feel an urgent need for certain kinds of action.

Against this background, international security arrangements have undoubtedly been growing in importance. They have taken many forms but can be broadly classified into three categories, each of which sets up its own political forces and has different implications for world security.

Formal treaties like the Kellogg Treaty,* the partial nuclear test ban or the non-proliferation treaty are, in effect, public legislative acts of the international order. They concentrate strong forces of support and opposition. Once negotiated, they create a fixed point from which they can be defended or against which opposition can be directed.

Informal arrangements can be stated or unstated and they will generally be confined to states which have an obvious interest in their subject matter. They are easy to reach and just as easy to abandon. It is probably true to say that they are the essential lubricants of any international order, covering everything from restraint in the deployment of fighting ships close to rival territory, to day-to-day life on a disputed frontier. But they have also been used to influence elements of

* The general treaty for the Renunciation of War, of 1928, known as the "Pact of Paris" or the "Kellogg–Briand Pact", was adhered to by 63 states.

security policy (like military budgets) which are of major significance.

Institutional structures are used for the administration of complex situations involving common action over a wide sphere. United Nations peace-keeping forces have been perhaps the outstanding examples, but institutions such as the International Atomic Energy Agency carry out major security responsibilities in the service of the international community as a whole.

Political attitudes towards arms control are inevitably conditioned by contemporary thinking about security problems. At present, it is possible to discern a divergence between public opinion and professional attitudes. Most governments reflect the view of their professional advisers that there are few really urgent security problems. In spite of their rhetoric, they believe in the existence of a stabilized balance of nuclear terror; they feel that a reasonable resolution of most security problems above the level of insurgency is more or less inevitable; and they are generally unwilling to become deeply concerned with longer-term problems of nuclear proliferation or new weapons—if only because governments do not think in the long term. Much public opinion, on the other hand, is hostile to the basic elements in the present order. It sees deterrence as a readiness to destroy mankind; it asks why there is no parallel in international society to the decline of physical power as the basis of domestic governments; and in many countries there is a strong awareness of wars that nobody wants to see repeated (Vietnam in the United States, the Second World War in the Soviet Union, Germany and Japan and the First World War among the older generation in France, Britain, Canada and Australia). In many cases, memories of war provide the popular emotional drive behind plans for world disarmament and world government which in one form or another most governments claim to support.

Governments have had to reconcile these optimistic and pessimistic schools—the one concerned about deterrence and the other about disarmament. This had been achieved in such countries as the United States, the Soviet Union and Britain by allowing the disarmers to make the proposals while the national security school makes the day-to-day policy. Each is content with this: generals do not like making proposals and political reformers do not usually know or care much about security. Success in keeping the balance has depended on the proposals for disarmament being so unrealistic that they did not threaten exclusive national control over security. Thus, the Soviet Government is able to propose general and complete disarmament in four years while simultaneously showing the gravest hesitation about a freeze on building new nuclear delivery systems; the far-reaching United States disarmament proposals enjoy the nominal support of those who are bitterly opposed to a ban on underground nuclear tests; British Governments precede Defence White Papers with solemn commitments to the great objective of disarmament while resisting agreements which might, for example, hold their stockpile of weapons-grade fissile material at its present substantial level. Governments which strain at the gnat of a modest international security arrangement easily swallow the camel of total nominal commitment to a disarmament they do not intend to permit.

This atmosphere has generated a reluctance to examine the political problems of international security negotiations. Most of the public advocacy of arms control and disarmament presumes that they are not only in the general interest but are by extension in the particular interest of any one government. This often leads to the conclusion that the real problem is to find the right political climate and that once this is achieved the agreements will be easy to negotiate. Yet it is obvious that arms control and disarmament agreements are in themselves difficult to reach and that most proposals provoke opposition among at least some powers. The interests of governments as they perceive them are difficult to reconcile; and they can only be resolved by building a consensus. When adequate support is not found and agreements are not reached, the orthodox reaction is to assume one of three things: that the international climate is not yet suitable; that certain governments are ignorant of their own interests; or that certain governments are acting in bad faith. Success in disarmament negotiations is thought to depend on getting over these barriers. Failures are therefore attributed either to the absence of a healthy international climate or to the ignorance of governments about their own and the world's interests. Hostility, or at least an inability to co-operate, is assumed to exist where there may merely be conflicts of interest; and some governments gain a reputation for ignorance or bad faith where this is not justified.

When, for one reason or another, there seems to be an improvement in the international climate or new men come into office, it is widely hoped that disarmament agreements will soon follow. The reality has proved and will prove very much more complex. The danger in assuming that agreements are necessarily in everyone's interest is that disappointment leads governments to underestimate what can be achieved in international security negotiations. The betrayal of false hopes can lead to resentment and a worsening of relations.

The presumption that these agreements are natural and only impeded by mistrust or ignorance can also be expected to have an effect once agreements are reached. It is assumed that agreements once made become a permanent part of the pattern of international life. Very little allowance is made for the possibility that they will become out of date, or be denounced, or become the target for political campaigns of various kinds. The image seems to be that the international order is gradually and more or less inevitably advancing, and that when it has captured a position it will hold and consolidate it. Little thought has been given to the problems of sustaining agreements once they develop security implications which no one took seriously at the time they were made, or the place the agreements might occupy in subsequent disputes between the parties to them. The agreements themselves could easily become targets of hostile opinion. Certainly their life after being negotiated can be just as political and just as difficult as the process of negotiation itself.

As with any specialized area of political life, international security will develop a tension between the technical facts and the political consensus. If there is a growing structure of international as well as national security, the international arrangements will have to live with technological and military change. The facts of power alter constantly and so do the men in power. At any one time those whose consent is necessary must have broadly the same appreciation of what these facts are. The politics of arms control is an attempt to keep two horses moving together: one is the altering nature of the problem of security; and the other is the changing character of what constitutes an effective consensus among the governments that are the world's security authorities. Many of the techniques for achieving this have been explored in the last two decades. Unfortunately, the wrong lessons have often been learned because expectations were pitched too high or the foundations were not effectively laid. We are dealing with an unexplored and unidealistic part of the political world which must, for certain purposes, be made to work. The nobility of the objective should not be allowed to obscure the inevitably rough political character of any consensus we manage to achieve.

There are four main types of arms control or disarmament agreement and each is likely to be negotiated in a different political context: (1) an agreement that does not essentially restrict weapons but constitutes, in effect, a rule of war; (2) an agreement that prevents an entirely new type of weapon from being produced; (3) an agreement that freezes the advantage of some powers and is openly discriminatory between powers; and (4) an agreement under which governments undertake to dismantle certain elements of their military power.

Agreements which are essentially rules of war have existed for many years. Perhaps the most important is the Geneva Protocol of 1925, which forbade the use of chemical and bacteriological weapons against other signatories. The Protocol has not prevented an accumulation of large stocks of these weapons; but as a point around which a general urge to restraint apparently converged it may have played a significant part in the European War between 1939 and 1945 and in other substantial conflicts since that time. While such weapons were used by the Italians in Ethiopia in 1935, by the Japanese in Manchuria in 1937, by the Egyptians in the Yemen in 1966, and by the United States in Vietnam in 1968–70,* the agreement itself and the long practice of abstention by many governments have undoubtedly served as a disincentive in many situations. The Soviet–American agreement not to station weapons of mass destruction in orbit or on the sea bed are also rules of war—and it can be expected to affect the normal peaceful dispositions of the armed forces of the two powers. The clause in the Latin American Non-Nuclear Zone Treaty forbidding all use of nuclear weapons similarly constitutes a rule of war. Such agreements are relatively easy to negotiate and can formalize a desire for restraint which all sides feel. War has always had rules and its changed character demands arrangements which are relevant.

The second kind of agreement—preventing new forms of weapons from being produced or created—has had some success in recent years. They are clearly easier to negotiate than agreements freezing an existing advantage or agreements which disarm. Because they are about something that governments have not yet decided to do, they possess no important element of discrimination between powers. But sustaining them may prove difficult if the military requirements change. Should certain possibilities denied under the agreements become progressively more attractive to defence planners, the pressure to renounce or evade the agreement can be expected to grow. A good example of this type of agreement would have been a restriction on the production of anti-ballistic missiles or multiple nuclear warheads before such weapons were produced in significant numbers—a possibility which has stirred considerable interest and in a modified form underlies the American approach to the Strategic Arms Limitation Talks (S.A.L.T.). We can expect those concerned with arms control to give thought to the application of this technique to virtually any new form of weapon.

An agreement of this kind has strong negotiating advan-

---

* The United States had not ratified the Protocol. Ratification was recommended to the Senate by President Nixon on 25 November 1969, but with a specific reservation on the non-lethal types of gas being used in Vietnam.

tages. For one thing, it arouses little domestic military opposition, which is a common source of resistance to arms control or disarmament agreements. Those branches of the armed forces which are equipped with bombers tend to construct arguments about the unique qualities of bombers. So do those with submarines, helicopters, tanks, artillery, long-range ballistic missiles, or any other existing weapon of war. Their resistance to change has been an important obstacle when, for various reasons, governments have tried to shift resources away from their technology. But where a new kind of military weapon is concerned, military advisers may even favour restricting it. Since the weapons *ex hypothesi* do not yet exist, no part of the armed forces has become dedicated to defending their importance. Tactical doctrines, rational or irrational, have not yet been constructed around them. Indeed, there is a considerable advantage to the military mind in preventing radical new changes in the nature of military force. In *status quo* powers, in particular, there is a natural fear that new weapons may destroy an existing advantage or upset a stabilized situation. Only anti-*status quo* powers welcome unpredictable strategic consequences, and in most circumstances even they are likely to have misgivings. For example, the prospect of bringing bacteriological weapons into warfare may conceivably be welcomed by some country which has undergone severe humiliation and is searching anxiously for something that will redress the power structure. But in general it is unlikely that any government in the world today is so anti-*status quo* as to want to allow the conscious spreading of disease to become a form of warfare.* Fear of the unfamiliar is also a powerful force working for bans on new weapons, just as the most powerful incentive in the original Anglo-American nuclear programme was undoubtedly the fear that the Ger-

---

* Although the United States began to stockpile weapons of this kind in the 1960s a full political-military analysis of the question at presidential level resulted in a statement in 1969 (by President Nixon) that the U.S. would never use such weapons, even in retaliation, and that all stocks were therefore being destroyed. This must be regarded as one of the great acts of sanity in our time.

mans might be ahead. The belligerent powers might well have agreed to ban atomic weapons in 1940 if they had had effective channels of negotiation and solid assurances that they could not be deceived. On the other hand, frustration on the Western Front had made most of the powers engaged in the First World War desperate to find a war-winning weapon—in effect, a means of breaching the military *status quo*. In this atmosphere, such radical innovations as poison gas and tanks were welcomed by orthodox soldiers as a means of ending a horrifying stalemate.

The domestic political context can, therefore, work in favour of arms control agreements that prevent the development of new weapons. When such measures are conservative they will enjoy the support of military conservatism. On the other hand, there must be serious concern on security grounds about stopping military innovation by agreement. Over many years, this practice is bound to create a substantial gap between what exists in the inventories of states and what might exist. A power starting behind and determined to break up the existing system (Germany and Japan in the 1930s; China in the 1970s) because it is politically unacceptable will be tempted to jump this widening gap. Thus many arms control agreements of this kind extended over a period of years could create a technical basis for an anti-*status quo* policy, leading the great powers to rest their security and that of the world order on weapons that would be ineffective in the face of a new challenge. A reinforcement of military conservatism by what is in effect an international legal structure could help to provoke the radical challenge which has so often brought disaster on forces organized according to the military principles which were effective in the preceding era.

There is also likely to be a problem of definition when the ban is on a class of weapon (like anti-ballistic missiles or space weapons) rather than an area of deployment (like nuclear weapons in Latin America or the demilitarization of the Antarctic). Agreements depend on words. If the agreements are reached in the infancy of the technology, the words used may well cease to mean what they were intended to mean. It would be interesting to speculate on the agreements which might have been based on a 1915 definition of tanks or a 1940 definition of atomic weapons (or super-bombs, as they were then being called).

The third main type of agreement freezes an existing situation in which some countries have certain weapons or military capabilities and others do not. Most proposals regarding nuclear weapons have fallen into this category. From the Soviet point of view, the Baruch Plan had this character: it would have forbidden the further development and construction of nuclear weapons at a time when the United States alone had tested weapons. In the same way, the partial nuclear test ban of 1963 and the Treaty on the Non-Proliferation of Nuclear Weapons of 1968 were and are openly discriminatory as between various powers. Their successful negotiation by a group of countries which included the United States and the Soviet Union is clearly due to the fact that neither of these was in the class being discriminated against.

This freeze type of agreement should also, in general, be comparatively easy to negotiate. The great powers themselves have an obvious incentive in confirming their own favourable position and in preventing others from equalling it. Since by definition the powers being favoured are likely to be the decisive ones at any given moment, the general international order can be expected to throw up agreements of this kind.

Sustaining such agreements is, however, equally certain to be difficult. The test ban had two challengers (France and China) from the start; the non-proliferation treaty aroused the concern and hostility of the next range of powers, though the two most immediately affected (West Germany and Japan) felt obliged to moderate their hostility because of the legacy of the Second World War and what they conceived to be the realities of their security position and international alignments. India, Sweden and others were more public in their objection to discrimination. This element inevitably weakens the moral basis of the great power position: and as, in time, the obligations of the treaty begin to limit what countries actually want to do (rather than what they might want to do in the future) the effects of this moral argument will grow more significant. These factors are often more important than those theoreticians of international relations who concentrate on national interests are likely to concede. An agreement such as a test ban obliges certain powers to desist from actions which the great powers have carried out and whose results continue to be of value to them. A non-proliferation treaty denies lesser powers weapons which the great powers regard as basic to their own security. Agreements of this kind can be sustained only if there is an important security relationship between those the treaty favours and those it inhibits. Certainly the attempt to force governments which are resisting or breaking such agreements into an unfavourable moral and political position has not succeeded—and is not likely to. The great power stance on nuclear testing, for example, has appeared too unconvincing to arouse public resentment of the French and Chinese tests.

The fourth type of agreement is the disarmament agreement which dismantles elements of existing military power. Most speculation about arms control concerns agreements of this kind, and many official proposals have, of course, been made for various types of disarmament. In spite of the prevailing conviction that we live in a perpetual arms race, governments regularly carry out decisions to disarm, usually because the value of troops or weapons does not seem to justify their cost and sometimes because of manpower shortages. But unless a disarmament agreement is simple and the objective well understood, disarmament by treaty is difficult to negotiate and, if negotiated, to carry out. After decades of effort, there are very few true examples of it.

There are a number of different approaches to all these types of agreement. They reduce themselves, however, to three basic types: formal agreements cast into treaties; informal agreements of various types, including tacit or unspoken arrangements; and the establishment of working institutions to administer certain areas of security policy jointly.

I *Formal Treaties*

Formal arms control and disarmament negotiations have generally looked towards treaties; and after arduous effort these have from time to time been achieved for particular purposes. Treaty negotiations can play an important part in political life in three distinct contexts: in their formulation as proposals; during the negotiation process; and in the destruction or denunciation of old agreements. Each of these has a quite different political character.

Treaty proposals. The formulation of proposals is significant in the domestic political life of many countries, though it appears to have little bearing on international politics at present. The Soviet Union felt the need to put forward broad and far-reaching plans for general disarmament from the Genoa Conference of 1922 to the Geneva Conference of 1932–34 and then again in the period after the Second World War. There can be two opinions about whether the Soviet Government would have agreed to such a programme of disarmament if others had accepted. The classic Lenin texts all spoke of disarmament before world revolution as a bourgeois notion. "While there is still oppression and exploitation on earth," he wrote in 1905, "we must strive not for disarmament, but for universal, popular armament." He held the same view in 1920 when he wrote that member parties of the International should fight against those who believed in "the League of Nations, disarmament and arbitration as means of averting wars". In recent years, however, the Russians have claimed that he dictated the line in favour of a general limitation of armaments which the Soviet negotiators took in Genoa in 1922.* There are differing opinions about whether the Soviets would have agreed to such a disarmament programme if others had accepted. What is obvious, however, is that the Soviet Government has known that there was no serious prospect of acceptance. They could therefore present their schemes for the political impact they were expected to

* There is a useful discussion of this history in Dallin et al., *The Soviet Union and Disarmament* (New York, Praeger 1964), chapter 9.

make. One objective was probably ideological, in the sense that a posture of this kind retained the notion of the withering away of state power as central to Soviet policy and thus helped to keep alive the principles of the revolution. More simply, G.C.D. was, as described by Mr. Khrushchev, "a potent weapon with which to rally the people".*

No other power has been quite so lavish in its disarmament proposals as the Soviet Union, although Britain also launched herself on G.C.D. in 1959 and the United States made its belated effort to catch up in 1962. The object in both cases was obviously political and the proposals were not intended for actual negotiation. It was hoped that domestic sentiment in favour of peace and disarmament would be appeased by putting the government's name to such far-reaching plans; and in the American case they were put forward by an administration which had previously attached considerable public significance to the formation of an independent Arms Control and Disarmament Agency (with the Director answerable directly to the President). Nevertheless, there is a strong domestic sentiment in the U.S. which is fearful of international security arrangements; and the United States would probably not have advanced its 1962 proposals if it had not felt the need to match the Soviet Union in what it took to be an international disarmament debate.

Britain and France made extensive disarmament and arms control proposals in the early 1950s. These were probably intended to lead to negotiation. As proposals, they were designed to show the desirable way forward in the event of much better East–West relations. The British effort to match the Soviet general disarmament proposal when it was made in 1959 was not, however, taken to the stage of a formal proposal.† They gave up their international role of disarmament

---

* Ibid., p. 121.

† The British Foreign Secretary, Mr. Selwyn Lloyd, made a statement in the U.N. General Assembly on 17 September 1959, the day before Mr. Khrushchev proposed that "over a period of four years all states should effect complete disarmament and should no longer have any means of waging war". Mr. Lloyd did not go quite so far. He said: "Our aim is to move forward by balanced stages towards the abolition

proposers in the 1960s when the United States asserted primacy in these matters in the Western Alliance.

Other countries have from time to time made proposals. Jawaharlal Nehru's India advocated various kinds of disarmament and was responsible for proposing the idea of a specific ban on nuclear testing in April 1954. India was at that time unwilling to accept the notion that there were major national security problems (beyond the manageable problem of Pakistan and such internal security issues as the pacification of Nagaland). Her proposals took the form of protests against any notion of a power system and reinforced the emotions that had given rise to the doctrine of non-alignment. This tradition has been continued by the non-aligned powers in the Geneva disarmament committee. No doubt this activity helps to give countries which feel excluded from the central direction of world affairs a sense of participation in world order. A posture of moral superiority is available to those who find this a satisfying compensation for their lack of influence. Countries availing themselves of this option are usually those in which a reputation for being men of peace is a valuable domestic political asset to prime ministers or foreign ministers.

States which consider themselves (and historically have considered themselves) to be secure and which therefore put little emphasis on the armed forces as their defenders are most inclined to take the lead in making arms control and disarmament proposals. The Americans, British, Swedes, Canadians, Irish, Mexicans and Brazilians are examples. India

---

of all nuclear weapons and all weapons of mass destruction and towards the reduction of other weapons and armed forces to levels which will rule out the possibility of aggressive war." But the actual proposals faltered. Admittedly, they said that the ultimate objective, or third stage, should be comprehensive disarmament by all powers under effective international control; but this was to be done by a ban on the manufacture and use of nuclear weapons and only "a re-examination of the possibility of controlling and then eliminating the remaining stocks of nuclear and other weapons of mass destruction". Perhaps the most striking fact about the Lloyd statement was the evidence it gave of Western intelligence on Soviet political intentions.

after 1962, Australia after 1941, and Israel throughout its short history are good examples of countries whose intellectual background might have led them to take a prominent stand in favour of disarmament but are inhibited by concern with national security problems.

It seems to be true for the present that a process of inflation (led by the Soviet Union) has largely destroyed the value of disarmament proposals as proposals. The Soviet–American competition reached levels of unreality in 1962 which seem to have removed all international political advantage from new and more extreme initiatives of this kind. More and more countries have also come to feel that their own capacity to defend themselves is important and that therefore far-reaching disarmament might not be entirely to their advantage. This no doubt explains the at least temporary disappearance of the disarmament proposal as a major ingredient of international politics after 1962.

Reaching formal agreements. The negotiation of formal international security agreements has also been a major element in the diplomatic life in our time and these have a different political context from the proposals which precede them. Proposals raise no risks, especially if it is assumed that they will be rejected. They seldom irrevocably commit the governments that make them. For one thing, few governments seriously believe that they will be taken up on their offers. Should they be, there are plenty of opportunities for seeing that any incautious elements in the proposal are modified or dropped in the process of negotiation. The unexpectedly favourable Soviet response in May 1955 to the group of American, British and French positions which had been developed between 1952 and 1955 led to a complete reservation of all American positions. Mr. Dulles' State Department showed an extraordinary lack of finesse in its hasty and disorderly retreat. But it is strange that the obvious conclusion should not have been drawn by such a close student of the problem as Mr. Philip Noel-Baker.* "Why did the (Western) Governments repudiate in September 1955 what they had

---

* *The Arms Race* (London, John Calder; New York, Oceana), pp. 28–30.

urged in 1952, 1953, 1954 and up to 10 May 1955?" he asks. He replies with further questions: "Has the thinking that inspired the United States policy of 1952–55 been eroded by the arms race? Have the United States Government reached the point reached by the British, French and Germans in 1914—do they now believe that only armaments can make them safe, and that 'keeping a lead' in weapons and in forces is the only way to safeguard the national interest and uphold the peace?" It did not apparently cross Mr. Noel-Baker's mind that the 1952–55 positions depended on Soviet refusal and that what had changed was the Soviet position. The Soviets were believed to be inviting a serious negotiation which up to then had been thought to be out of the question.

Reaching agreements brings into play all the fears of those who will be restricted. Here one passes from the public relations side of foreign policy to the heart of security policy and so to the most vital concerns of governments. When, as is common, many countries are involved, interests will vary and their reconciliation will require a major effort. These negotiations provide those who are resisting the international *status quo*, for example, with something they can safely oppose and even scorn. Governments such as the French and Chinese in the middle and late 1960s had no desire or ability to challenge the *status quo* by force. But a nuclear test ban (which would affect them) or a non-proliferation treaty (which would not) gave them good opportunities to show their unwillingness to participate in an order whose general character or leadership they did not like. Equally, a negotiation for a non-proliferation treaty or (as has not taken place) one of the Soviet, Polish or British plans for freezing or reducing forces in Central Europe can create an area of open dispute with a country like West Germany, which is otherwise reluctant to provoke a conflict with the great powers. Rivalries come to the surface which might otherwise have remained quiescent. The Non-Proliferation Treaty was an obvious source of irritation between the United States and West Germany and this was undoubtedly one reason for Soviet interest in its negotiation.

Agreements which are achieved have a variety of positive functions. Unlike proposals which are intended to be rejected, they give evidence of the ability of rival powers to work together; and while nothing so far negotiated or likely to be negotiated has had the function of "reducing tension", all agreements have convinced the powers concerned that they can work together and that within limits their rivals are rational men. This creates a sense that problems can be solved. It strengthens patience in periods of hostility. The achievement of agreements adds real, if temporary, strength to the international order, quite apart from whatever substantive changes are made from the working of the agreement.

In domestic terms, there is much more to be gained from achieving a treaty than from simply making proposals. In countries like Britain and the United States, the peace plank in the electoral platform can be important and valuable; and the electorate can no longer be taken in by plans. The British Conservative Government fought hard for the partial nuclear test ban treaty for electoral purposes and subsequently derived real electoral benefits from it. The American Democratic administration considered that the Non-Proliferation Treaty was a valuable contribution to its 1968 election campaign. On the other hand, governments do not want to be exposed to the charge that in some element of national security they have been deceived by rivals, or even by friends. The security case must be made and proved—particularly in those countries in which security issues actively concern the public.

Sustaining agreements. Once an agreement is reached, it can be expected to pass from the active political scene. Its importance becomes military: that is to say, it is as important as its continuing security content. The conclusion of the treaty prohibiting the use in war of asphyxiating, poisonous or other gases, or the partial nuclear test ban, or the agreements not to put vehicles of mass destruction in outer space or on the sea bed, no doubt had an effect on international life and also had important domestic effects. But once the agreements were made they had very little political content. They dropped below the level of active political discussion and dispute and they ceased to influence the range of hostilities and friendships in the world.

This situation can, however, change at any time. One or more governments can choose to bring a treaty back into the political arena—for either political or military reasons. There are times when domestic popularity can be courted by a vigorous attack on some symbol of the inevitable restrictions of the international order; or some new security argument or military development might deprive an agreement of its *raison d'être* for one or more states. There is an obvious risk in agreements which were entered into primarily because they would contribute to a better international atmosphere at a time when this was obviously desirable. Years pass and the climate changes. The agreement ceases to have any relevance to the political purpose for which it was designed. If its security content was originally small, there will never have been a strong incentive to maintain it. But whether it was small or large, the situation will almost inevitably change. From time to time, therefore, most governments will find themselves inconvenienced by arms control or disarmament agreements. We can expect them to bring these agreements back into international political life through the invocation of escape clauses, by reinterpretations* which others will find unacceptable, or by simple denunciation.

* An excellent example of what can happen is provided by the evolution of the attitude of the United Kingdom Government to the Protocol for the Prohibition of the Use in War of Asphyxiating, Poisonous or other Gases, and of Bacteriological Methods of Warfare, signed at Geneva, 17 June 1925. The parties to this accepted a prohibition on "the use in war of asphyxiating, poisonous or other gases, and of all analogous liquids, materials or devices". Ambiguities were soon detected about the use of screening smoke in war and also the use of various gases in internal security situations. In a parliamentary reply in 1930 the British Government defined its position on these: "Smokescreens are not considered as poisonous and do not, therefore, come within the terms of the Geneva Gas Protocol. Tear gases and shells producing poisonous fumes are, however, prohibited under the protocol." This view was generally accepted. When, however, the extensive use of CS gas, a highly effective riot-control agent, was decided on by the British Government in Northern Ireland, and when American military experience of CS in Vietnam proved attractive, a new definition was

There are so few disarmament and arms control treaties that so far this has not been an important element in international life. But the growth of a series of formal agreements on the precedents which now exist could make security treaties a central factor in domestic security thinking and in international life. Had the rapid changes in weapons and military organization of the 1950–65 period been made against an involved mass of legal inhibitions (as with the naval programmes of the 1930s), different decisions would have been taken by some powers; and undoubtedly an important new source of international dispute would have been created. Just as unwarranted assumptions about the strength of the international order can be drawn from the negotiation of agreements, so quite unrealistic fears may be raised by their denunciation. Governments which have not grasped the security reasoning which is leading rivals to evade or denounce a treaty will see the most sinister implications. Certainly they will take the opportunity to make political capital (as the West did over the Soviet breach in the moratorium on nuclear testing in 1961).

Treaties are thus likely to run into difficulties in the face of changes in weapons, tactics and military appreciations. A change of men, either in the high command or in the political leadership, may be enough to deprive a treaty of its support. But there is another important issue which is entirely political in character—namely, the value of a breach in an arms control or disarmament treaty as a political end in itself. Those who speculate on disarmament subjects normally assume that all governments always want a reputation for being peaceful and well-intentioned, even when they are not. But some recognition should be given to the government which wants a reputation for toughness and belligerence, often when it is

---

unilaterally offered. In a written parliamentary reply, the Foreign Secretary said: "Modern technology has developed CS smoke which, unlike the tear gases available in 1930, is considered to be not significantly harmful to man in other than wholly exceptional circumstances; and we regard CS and other such gases accordingly as being outside the scope of the Geneva Protocol." (House of Commons Debates, 2 February 1970, cols. 17–18).

in no position to do anything really tough or belligerent. Indeed, a deep sense of frustration, of being able to do nothing, generally gives rise to this phenomenon. Already we have had many examples of frustration in the face of an order which is capable of humiliating quite substantial powers. The Soviet Union was humiliated over Berlin (after issuing an ultimatum) in the summer of 1961; and its need to show some kind of defiance in order to save face may well have been an element in its decision to break dramatically with the moratorium on nuclear tests (a direct breach of a Soviet undertaking, though not of a treaty). Britain and France were humiliated over Suez in 1956; and it is possible to attribute many of the attitudes and actions of both countries since that time to the psychology this produced.

Anyone who studies security problems in our day will be impressed with the extent to which all powers are continuously searching for actions that will make an impact on others but which are nevertheless safe in the sense that they are unlikely to start a chain of actions over which there can be no effective control. Because the direct conflict of large organized fighting formations appears potentially uncontrollable, this has comparatively seldom been used as an instrument of policy. A structure of arms control agreements (together with inspectors and limitations of various kinds) is a safe and standing target for those who are anxious to express hostility to the world order. Denunciation thus opens up a range of political options. Governments may threaten to abrogate some part of the system or they may actually denounce all or part of an arms control structure. It must be recognized that such a structure will be a standing attraction to countries that feel that they have been treated unjustly. In a world in which military options have declined, anything that might serve as a suitable substitute is likely to be pressed into action from time to time.

Taken all in all, the treaty is the great public occasion of the arms control and disarmament field. Governments must respond in public to its provisions and the suspicious defenders of national security will invariably ask why the country's adversaries are so interested in it. This is a particular problem in the United States, where treaties must be ratified by a two-thirds majority in the Senate and where there will usually be critical hearings. The Non-Proliferation Treaty negotiations have shown how a proposed treaty with security implications can instigate important political debates and form political attitudes in many countries. For this reason, treaties are probably the best way to achieve domestic political benefits from international security undertakings, if it is these that are sought. Governments claiming to be the sponsors of peace policies can gain the maximum advantage if their leaders can show that they have played a significant part in their negotiation.

Apart from a treaty's dramatically public character, its outstanding characteristic is that of definition. It uses words which are public and which both sides have accepted. As has been argued, these words might prove to be less clear with the passage of time and the development of technology; but at least there is no doubt what the words were and there is generally no great doubt about the original intention. Treaties also offer an excuse for responding to a violation since they give other powers a basis from which to object to actions forbidden by the agreement. A treaty can thus be a valuable ally to those elements in a governmental debate which oppose whatever it forbids. Few security treaties, of course, contain any enforcement provision. Such provisions could become a dangerous source of international conflict and are by no means necessarily desirable. In obvious cases like the Soviet violation of the partial nuclear test ban in January 1965, the American violation in December 1970 or the Egyptian use of gas in the Yemen, there has been little response.

The function of the treaty is therefore overwhelmingly political. Its attractions are political and so are the objections to it. Those who are professionally concerned with achieving international security arrangements distrust them. This is especially true in the United States, where there is anxiety not to have to face constant battles with congressional and military advocates of national security. Both the United States and the Soviet Union have difficulty in their various ways in arriving at treaties; France and China object in principle to security treaties; and for these reasons the treaty is likely to be a limited instrument in the coming years.

II *Informal agreements*

Informal agreements can be purely tacit, based on a calculated series of responses to the actions of others; they can be unofficially agreed through the discussions of officials at various levels; and they can have more precision and strength through agreed minutes of conversations. There always have been and always will be many informal agreements of great importance to security. Wherever troops have been in contact in peacetime, for example, it has been normal that certain agreed practices should be established. Radio, radar, space, electronics, modern reconnaissance methods, and many other factors have forced a broad increase in this type of understanding.

There are many advantages in informal agreements and every reason to believe that they will become more common as the years go on. Their political content is minimal and so they allow mutual security considerations to predominate. To the extent that they solve genuine security problems, they strengthen the hand of those who favour international security arrangements in domestic political and bureaucratic debates. If it can be argued by a school of opinion in Washington or Moscow that to take account of the other side's interest in various informal ways will lead to certain favourable actions in response, and if these actions then take place, the advocates of moderation and co-operation will gain in strength. It is now a commonplace of American strategic argumentation that much can be done in just this way to strengthen the Soviet doves in their disputes with the Soviet hawks.

American interest in this approach has been greatly stimulated by the desire to achieve some form of limitation on strategic nuclear armaments. While this is a major national objective officially sponsored by two Administrations, there is obvious anxiety about restraints which are too formal or too permanent. Uncertainty remains about the technological future and also about China and other powers. The attraction of informal understandings is that they can be annulled or altered in new situations and that therefore no security commitment is being made into an unknown future. A good example was the American Soviet informal agreement to limit their defence budgets. The United States dropped this quietly but completely when the Vietnam conflict imposed drastic increases. To the Americans, this was an unforeseen circumstance; to the Soviets, a breach of the agreement. But to both it was clear evidence that an informal agreement is only as enduring as the obvious interest which made it possible. Similarly, informal agreements about the level of forces in central Europe would have been abandoned by the Soviet Union in the face of the situation produced by the policies of the Dubcek government in Czechoslovakia. An informal agreement is, in effect, conditional: if unforeseen and unexpected circumstances emerge (and only the government concerned can be the judge of this) the agreement is off. Many things may be possible on this basis which would be impossible on any more formal basis.

The case for informal agreements has been developed primarily by government officials and by members of the academic world whose links with governments are at the official level. It is among these people that we have had a striking growth in recent years of a kind of freemasonry— international links at a level which is distinct from the politicians, from the party organizations and from the military commands. Informal agreements, being at a level which does not impinge on politics, have a strong appeal to this official class, whose power over policy is steadily growing.

It happens that in both the United States and the Soviet Union academic and semi-academic institutions have developed with access to classified information and government finance, and with a semi-official status. The people in these institutions, together with appropriate government officials, are well placed to initiate and sustain dialogues at a nominally unofficial level. These can and do lead to a common mind and to mutually supporting policies. This development owes much to American effort and reflects the familiar American belief in the virtue of the dialogue and the advantages of personal ties. It has proved its value in the long-standing links between senior scientists, particularly in the field of atomic energy, and is being extended in the Soviet Union through official support of institutional developments like the Institute of the United States of America.

We must recognize, however, that informal agreements raise considerable difficulties. The undoubted advantages of minimizing the domestic political element in arms control agreements have parallel disadvantages. These may prove more severe in the long run. Serious complications may emerge at a later date if major decisions on security policy have been taken because of informal agreements. The circumstances are not hard to imagine. If, during one of the perennial panics over some arms gap or other, testimony was given (for example) by American military planners that restraint had been shown because of informal agreements with the Soviet Union, the administration could be put in a very embarrassing position. The revelation that significant parts of defence planning had become subject to secret and informal agreements with rival governments could arouse elemental fears in Congress or the electorate. Those who had promoted such arrangements might find they were in a difficult position. In a subsequent period of recrimination the line between valuable informal agreements and conspiring with the enemy might be very difficult to demonstrate. Officials and their academic allies would like to operate in a world in which the irrationalities of politics can be minimized. The desire for informal agreements is part of this wholly proper professional prejudice. But in developing the international character of their part of the security process they should not make the error of thinking that they can create a world independent of politics.

There is a further problem. If treaties suffer from the difficulty of fixed words which may gradually lose relevance or precise meaning, informal agreements have the opposite failing: they can easily be the subject of serious misunderstandings as to precisely what was agreed. Lawyers and businessmen know this difficulty, even when working in a single language on subjects which are by no means vital. This problem is compounded by the complexity of the security field and the number of different authorities which carry out policy. Agreements will be made in the context of international meetings where compromises are reached; but they will be carried out in an entirely national environment on each side. There can be a gap between what was said in the international atmosphere and what is done by a national administration. This gives rise to a serious danger: one or both sides can easily come to feel betrayed by the other. Informal agreements (unless they are tacit) usually involve an element of trust. Assurances are given by those who must later face domestic pressures from the military, from sections of the bureaucracy or from political forces. They cannot easily bring the language and mentality of their international dialogue to those whose arguments are conducted in a narrower (or at any rate, different) atmosphere. If, as is likely, what is finally done falls significantly short of what the other side thought was agreed, there will be a feeling that the agreement was not entered into in good faith. The danger of a sense of deception, of a belief that the rival is unprincipled and untrustworthy, is immensely destructive in international life. It was what he conceived to be "deliberate deception" which particularly inflamed President Kennedy during the 1962 Cuban missile crisis.* The conviction that no form

* This provides an interesting illustration of the problem of words in security undertakings. In his celebrated television speech to the American people of 22 October 1962, in which he declared a quarantine on Soviet ships going to Cuba, President Kennedy quoted what he called the false statements of the Soviet Government in its statement of 11 September. The specific quotations given by him were: "The armaments and military equipment sent to Cuba are designed exclusively for defensive purposes. . . . There is no need for the Soviet Union to shift its weapons . . . for a retaliatory blow to any other country, for instance Cuba. . . . The Soviet Union has so powerful rockets to carry these nuclear warheads that there is no need to search for sites for them beyond the boundaries of the Soviet Union." It is easy to see how President Kennedy believed he had been deceived. It is also easy to see how it could be held that each of these statements was in its literal meaning true.

of arrangement could be made with such people informed such diverse relations as those between Britain and France (on the one hand) and the Soviet Union in 1939, India and Pakistan during the first 15 years of independence, the Allied and Axis powers in the Second World War, Britain and Egypt in 1956, and so on. Almost invariably these attitudes can be traced back to bitterness at breaches of what one side took to be trust. This mistrust goes far beyond the subject matter of the alleged breach. They lead to a contempt and hostility which can be a prime cause of international crisis and war.

Informal agreements are also difficult to operate for any substantial number of countries. The favour which they have gained in Washington is to some extent due to the conviction that the only important area of arms control negotiations at present is with the Soviet Union. Britain (it is assumed) can be brought along; France and China (it is argued) are unwilling to negotiate about anything, formally or informally: Germany, Japan, India and others (it is hoped) do not yet matter enough to be decisive. There is a dangerous simplicity in this. A consensus of two may be adequate for the moment on such issues as restraint in A.B.M. or multiple warhead development; but it will have to be steadily broadened. It is noticeable that the tendency to drop Britain from the consensus is having an effect on British identification with the *status quo*. West Germany and Japan could both become very difficult for the major powers to handle in a period of exclusive and growing Soviet-American *détente* in which little effort was made to accommodate them. Agreements affecting nuclear weapons will be limited in effect so long as China and France are outside them; agreements which are to affect Europe, the Middle East, Asia or any other major area must include the main powers in the region; naval agreements must incorporate the main maritime powers; and even space is gradually being occupied by a number of powers in addition to the original two. Informal agreements on this broader basis will be difficult to achieve and sustain.

Some kinds of agreement will be more difficult because of the lack of any assurance that they will survive for long. It is in the nature of the informal agreement that it is not binding even in the sense that governments are in some way publicly committed to it. Such agreements will therefore be about what is, rather than what will be, and their most useful function may be to give evidence through informal verification that they are being respected.

Finally, it must be objected that informal agreements lay no foundations on which an international order can be built. To the extent that they succeed, their success is likely to go undetected. One of the observable realities of politics—and one of the strongest elements in any enduring political order—is that public loyalty develops towards those who over a period of time provide security. Whether it is the Soviet or German Army, the British Navy or the American nuclear force, it is evident that within the political system there was a readiness to support these agents, or supposed agents, of national security. Law and government enjoy general support because they hold back the forces of chaos. In international life, a deep identification with the League of Nations was observable in many governments and people when there was a belief that it would keep the peace. A similar attachment to the United Nations persists in many places today. It is therefore a reasonable presumption that to the extent that security is genuinely achieved through agreement, political support for the agencies of that security will grow. Informal agreements, however, offer no such object to the public view. They are potentially a useful reinforcement of national security systems (if they do not endanger a security by creating, from time to time, a sense of betrayal) but they do not exploit their own longer-term political potential. If successful, they will merely credit national security systems with achieving results which will have depended to a considerable extent on the obscure means by which the informal agreements with rivals were achieved.

These objections do not amount to a case against informal agreements. But as with treaties, they suggest that there are limits to their usefulness. To go into a large number of informal arrangements will require a level of understanding between or among governments which does not exist and is unlikely to develop. But the freemasonry of the Pugwash movement and the international dialogue of the political-military community is forming one of the essential foundations on which the reform of power can be built. It is leading people to offer in private the rationale of their security behaviour and so (where deception is not involved) to make international security thinking possible. The growth of a range of informal agreements could broaden the base of national security thinking provided everyone concerned realized that for states as for individuals it is unwise to put your trust in princes.

III *Institutions*

In the period since the Second World War there has been a remarkable acceleration in the setting up of international institutions. They range from the political to the technical and from the nearly universal to comparatively narrow groups of countries. In the security field, at least one formal alliance structure, the North Atlantic Treaty Organization, has enjoyed remarkable success and prestige while a number of others have survived through changing circumstances. The United Nations, like the League of Nations, reflects in its Charter the conviction of victorious wartime allies that they should collectively keep the peace, claiming where threats to the peace were involved a total right of intervention. Article 1 of the Charter states: "The Purposes of the United Nations are:

"1. To maintain international peace and security, and to that end: to take effective collective measures for the prevention and removal of threats to the peace, and for the suppression of acts of aggression or other breaches of the peace . . ."

Article 42 states: " . . . (The Security Council) may take such action by air, sea or land forces as may be necessary to maintain or restore international peace and security . . ."

The organization has not, of course, come close to fulfilling the tasks given to it by its founders. The Security Council's vast paper powers of enforcement have so far been confined to preventing one ship of doubtful registry from entering the Port of Beira at a time when there were still strong hopes about the effect of sanctions on an independent Rhodesia. The Committee of 33 (the Special Committee on Peace-keeping Operations) has lacked the strength and coherence to deal with the *ad hoc* peace-keeping function which has been accepted by the world organization. The Conference of the Committee on Disarmament (together with its various predecessors) has not attempted to achieve any real professional competence in the security field and has devoted itself largely to mutual and generally accurate accusations by the Soviet and Western *blocs* that the other is not really interested in disarmament. At times it has provided a useful forum for the discussion of various disarmament and arms control measures; but as a security institution the C.C.D. has no serious standing at all.

The institutional record in security matters over the last quarter of a century is therefore one of constant effort, little progress, and yet of surviving institutions. In most crises, the United Nations has been expected to act, or at least to provide its services in the pursuit of agreement. It enjoys the tribute of universal dissatisfaction and remains in some way the repository of hope. There may be a case for trying to set up entirely new security institutions, especially if it is believed that institutional development will only be possible with a selective membership. But the U.N. has retained its claim on *prima facie* consideration for any development of international security institutions by the surviving fact of the Charter, the basic loyalty to it of most governments* and its real achievements in certain international security crises. Any attempt to develop such institutions will require a structure which can evolve its own professionalism and at the same time build up an effective consensus among governments for policies designed to increase international security. Though their institutions vary widely, modern governments have all had the problem of achieving a balance between the professional

* The main exceptions are China, France and South Africa, with their various spheres of influence. This is an important but perhaps not decisive group.

advisers of the executive and the political compromisers who must in the end be brought along.

To build up and maintain a professional body in which security problems could be analysed from an international point of view would be a delicate political exercise. Although its ultimate function would be to shape the security policies of states, this function would have to be developed discreetly and with great sympathy for the objects of national policies. No country is going to support an institution which, in its view, is devoted to questioning the essential objectives of its own security policies. On the other hand, most governments have an interest in seeing how the same security can be obtained more cheaply and more certainly through common action.

Some institutions with these characteristics have been built up by the non-Communist world to deal with the very difficult and conflicting problems presented by economic policy. It is true that the participants have been states committed to public expressions of mutual goodwill and have been bound (generally speaking) by formal alliances. It has nevertheless also been true that some of the subjects which the International Monetary Fund (I.M.F.), the Organization for Economic Cooperation and Development (O.E.C.D.), the General Agreement on Tariffs and Trade (G.A.T.T.), and the Group of Ten have successfully managed on a multilateral basis are of intense and conflicting political interest— in real terms often more so than the security policies of countries in the kind of frozen rivalry which exists between N.A.T.O. and the Warsaw Pact. The western economic institutions have achieved such remarkable results because there were broad acknowledged common objectives and a will to make the institutions work.

In the economic field, finance ministers have come to know each other and professionals have developed a body of common argument about economic policy in various countries, as expressed in the published studies of the O.E.C.D.*
and still more (it is said) in the unpublished studies of the I.M.F. It is difficult to see why a skilled professional group of

* See chapter 5.

international security servants should not produce studies of national security policy on the authority of the institution. The central bankers have achieved at least some capacity to act in common when their political masters require it. On other less urgent issues (the long-debated subject of liquidity, for example), the international financial mechanisms work slowly to achieve a consensus. States divide into different parties defending different points of view and each has its academic and scholarly champions. From time to time an international problem becomes so acute that it is obvious that certain things must be done. The consensus which was lacking is built up behind a position which had previously been advocated but with inadequate support. Majorities are made and unmade for particular purposes. This takes place against a background of critical activity by international and national specialists who are in close touch both with the international staff and with their opposite numbers in other countries. The complex facts of the situation are constantly seen from a multilateral point of view. From long habit, national decisions over anything to do with trade, aid, the valuation of the currency, tariffs, or any one of many other subjects are automatically reviewed for their effects on the international economic order as represented by the regulations and policies of the collective institutions. Governments have become responsive to the objection by their professional advisers that a given course of action would meet with international disapproval. The hands of those advocating policies most in line with agreed international policies are also inevitably strengthened. The entire structure depends, of course, on a basic reasonableness on the part of all governments. Obviously there is by no means general agreement in any one case on what is reasonable; and all countries from time to time act in a way that many or all others consider unreasonable. But many of those concerned, national and international, contemplating the same facts and enduring the same experiences, do eventually develop a sense of what is reasonable in the situations that really matter.

In any effort to develop institutions dealing specifically with security, membership is basic. To gain strength and attract support, an institution has to go on for many years evolving its methods of work, its acknowledged rules of action and its style. It must become accepted, recognized and even to some extent loved. It must evolve a kind of servant which corresponds to its political context and the expertise it requires. All this is the acknowledged stuff of life in any successful political organization, whether local, national or international. One of the advantages of western economic institutions has been that they have on the whole been limited to states which were ready and able to meet certain rules. They are the creatures of the like-minded. Power in trade and finance is also an evident and immediate thing and there has been no tendency for the institutions to fall under the control of those who were not really predominant. In spite of the lively intervention of the poor in the trade field through the United Nations Conference on Trade and Development (U.N.C.T.A.D.), institutions formed on this basis can scarcely become the repositories of real political power or influence.

There is a genuine difficulty in reconciling the need for continuity in institutions with the fact that some countries are from time to time unwilling to join in any reasonable consensus. N.A.T.O. worked effectively over a wide range of security issues on the basis of its anti-Communist membership of the 1950s; but when France withdrew her support the institution lost much of its capacity to act. In the opposite sense, the attempts to work the U.N. machinery at a time when the Soviet Union and the West were in deep and basic conflict led to pessimistic assumptions about the security value of the U.N. Mainly as a result of Soviet policy, the U.N. was not allowed to develop expertise in security; and there is a feeling that the institution itself has failed and cannot do in the future what it has been unable to accomplish in the past. In any case, there must be serious doubts about the effectiveness of an institution with its membership and constitution. Nevertheless, the reason for its past failures would seem to be the reverse of the reason for N.A.T.O.'s successes: it has had a membership which was too deeply divided to achieve a common security effort. That has now probably changed where the principal actors, the United States and the Soviet Union, are concerned, at least in a preliminary way.* It remains to be seen whether the accumulated failure and scepticism of the years will make it impossible for the U.N. to draw strength from this new reality. It may have unusual difficulty in giving life to a consensus which is potentially there and which it is the function of a good international institution to discover and exploit.

Given such limitations, it is reasonable to expect the first developments to come from a smaller group of powers, presumably surrounding the United States and the Soviet Union. A pattern can already be discerned in the Soviet–American–British negotiation of the partial nuclear test ban (followed by widespread adherence), the Soviet–American negotiation of the non-proliferation treaty (followed by the signatures of a less broad range of states and many qualifications about ratification), and the Soviet–American Strategic Arms Limitation Talks. The use of the N.A.T.O. and Warsaw Pact organizations during both the N.P.T. and the S.A.L.T. negotiations is clearly important and could bring life into N.A.T.O., in particular, in a new sphere of action. Alliances such as these have the advantage of unified staffs expert in security; and they have shown some capacity to reach decisions in common if that is really necessary. In parliamentary terms, the alliances may have some of the functions of the whips which see that the voting power goes into the lobbies. But this relationship works two ways. If the whips are to be able to recruit the votes they must also provide the machinery by which those who have developed the habit of co-operation with the system are able to influence what happens, within the limits of their power.

On security issues, the United Nations has made little contribution to this consensus-building; but in recent years it has made some interesting efforts to mobilize professional advice in these matters. The preliminaries to the nuclear test

* These two powers have developed an interesting inner dialogue in the Conference of the Committee on Disarmament where as co-chairmen they have begun to exercise a powerful joint influence. The first elements of resistance to this are becoming evident among the other members of the conference, both aligned and non-aligned.

ban were instructive. Scientists from many countries drew up a joint analysis of the requirements for an enforced ban on testing, and negotiations then took place on issues which were both technical and political. A similar technique with a less clear-cut objective was used by the General Assembly in recommending to the Secretary-General that studies be done on the economic consequences of disarmament, the effects of nuclear weapons and chemical and bacteriological weapons. These were then produced by committees with representatives from 12 countries. The results can scarcely be considered to be significant from the security point of view, but they are part of the process of raising the common factor of knowledge and information. This body of accepted fact and argument can then be used as a basis for further study and debate and as a point of reference for policy.

An institutional approach to this kind of thing can avoid political complications. Even sensitive governments have been glad to join in these studies because they felt they could influence the report in the direction of their national policy. In contrast, when the United States invited the Soviet authorities to join in their seismic tests for the verification of underground nuclear tests off the Kurile islands, and to the opening of the large aperture seismic array in Montana, the Soviet authorities declined. They could sense (no doubt with reason) the American effort to implicate them in technical assessments which would help to justify the American line on underground tests. It is not going to be easy in any context to develop regular technical appreciations which governments will not fear. But the best hope is an international institution founded on respect for national defence concerns and sensitive to those issues which governments feel are important.

On technical subjects whose political content is reasonably small, there may be promise in the development of agencies on the model of U.S. government agencies. The International Atomic Energy Agency, in spite of its slow and troubled development, is an excellent example. It is conceivable that agencies might begin joint work on weather technologies or oceanography; and there is much basic arms control research which would be far more usefully done internationally. Some joint western activity has been sponsored by the Americans. Project Cloudgap, for example, included a joint Anglo-American test in Britain to see what problems are raised by the inspection of retained levels of forces under a disarmament agreement. Obviously there will be security problems in including adversaries in this type of research; but it goes without saying that no results will be of benefit if they are not accepted by the Soviet Union and other parties to any agreement to reduce forces. It is hard to imagine the Soviet Union inviting Americans to take part in work of this kind. But it is not at all difficult to foresee field studies being done by an international security institution, extending the methods used in the existing U.N. studies deeper and deeper into the world security structure.

Institutions also have an important function in developing support for particular policies. Any consensus has to be built through the familiar techniques of pressure and compromise on which all political systems are based in one way or another. In successful political institutions many opinions are finally concentrated on particular actions. The advantage of an international institution for this purpose is that what has to be done can be done without being impeded by the persistent if obsolete notion that sustained co-operation between adversaries is impossible. Americans and Russians still have difficulty in reaching an agreement together and carrying it out; so do Indians and Pakistanis, Israelis and Arabs, South Africans and most others, Indonesians and Malaysians, and so on. Neighbouring hostilities will be a continuing part of international life. An institution with an understood life and set of loyalties of its own can act independently of these local political rivalries.

Establishing international security institutions would therefore seem to be the most important objective in laying the foundation for a reform of power. We shall face an inevitable tension between the need for consensus and the determination of the major powers not to operate through institutions where those who do not really matter can make a nuisance of themselves. This is really the process of deciding how important everyone is; and resolving this acceptably will inevitably make enormous demands on the skill of those responsible for the development of the institution. A barnyard is no doubt at its worst when the hens have not established their pecking order. If a consensus is to be built up for specific purposes, it must be preceded by a general sense of how much influence the various elements may have.

An institution which can solve these difficult but universal problems and evolve an effective professional life has a number of advantages over treaties or informal agreements:

1. It makes common research and experiment possible on a continuing basis, thus helping to develop a common outlook in the security thinking of the powers. It is a dubious assumption that the specialists really understand each other. At even the most sophisticated level, there appear to be major differences in thought and terminology between, for example, the Warsaw Pact and N.A.T.O. countries.

2. Its professionals will be of incalculable value in building and sustaining the peace. As in national affairs, such men might be expected to emerge in scientific, military or political-military roles. The Soviets can be expected to take longer than most to get used to having some of their trusted men work in a larger context and develop a broader outlook; and progress in the reform of power will have to wait for this evolution in Soviet attitudes. But the best way to get this evolution is to prove through experience that the working of security institutions serving world interests is to the security advantage of the Soviet Union. An incidental advantage would be that the men who had served in this special context would be of real value to Soviet policy when they return to national defence and other establishments. These considerations apply in many other cases besides that of the Soviet Union, though the Soviet case is perhaps the most important.

3. Its political life will offer a new medium for the development of politicians with a reputation for being men of peace. One of the achievements of the League of Nations was that it provided political figures such as Jules Moch, Anthony Eden or Jan Smuts with an international forum in which they could build world reputations as international statesmen.

The United Nations offered a context for some national political figures—Mr. Lester Pearson is perhaps the outstanding example—during the high days of the Hammarskjöld peace-keeping efforts: but it seems true to say that no politician of consequence is at present building his career on a position as an international statesman dedicated to a better world order. The reputation of political figures is one of the elements which makes political institutions work, providing as it does the link between complex policies and broad public trust. They are also invaluable in responding to a crisis.

4. It can avoid becoming frozen in the technology of the day. It should be possible to form and reform its outlook, rules and policies in relation to technical and military change.

5. As the effective consensus for particular purposes changes, adaptable and wisely run institutions will be able to broaden the working system (to the extent that there is one) to include those who must be brought in as partners. An institution may fail to adapt itself to the pretensions of new powers, especially if its principal members decide to use it to try to preserve their privileged position; but at least it has the potential for adaptation.

6. To the extent that international security is achieved, and is seen to be achieved, the institutions which have made it possible will attract both loyalty and expectations. This should increase their ability to handle future problems.

7. Institutions give trusted men the opportunity to create a consensus where this must be an artifice developed in relation to need. Security has always been the responsibility of men. A Hammarskjöld, an Eisenhower or a Norstad can enjoy a general trust in a group of countries that could never be commanded for any particular element of their policy. In a really dangerous international security crisis, the importance of having such men with a broadly based professional staff under them cannot be exaggerated. The need for them will be greatest where nuclear weapons are about to be used, or have been used, or where in other ways governments have become the prisoners of events.

These considerations point strongly to the need to move

from the stage of formal and informal agreements to working machinery for the reform of power. Unlike the Commonwealth of Massachusetts, which with admirable impartiality proclaims itself a government of laws and not of men, the administration of security has always been a matter of men and not of laws. Elaborate treaties growing older cannot be expected to handle the complications which international security arrangements will produce. Even the subjects already included in international security treaties—nuclear tests, nuclear proliferation, chemical and bacteriological weapons, nuclear weapons in orbit, the Antarctic—raise complex and changing issues. The agreements were reached because they passed the political tests of their day. The problem of keeping them going is already one of great complexity.

There is therefore a clear need for a conscious beginning on the construction of an international security authority. If possible, it should have the following characteristics:

1. It should not undermine what the powers now regard as the sources of their security.

2. It should give the whole world, and especially the middle powers, a direct share in their own security.

3. It should gain the capacity to control the evolution of weapons so as (*a*) to maintain a stable second strike nuclear confrontation and (*b*) to stop the development of cheap systems of mass destruction.

4. It should have such control over existing weapons of mass destruction that the dangers of accident will be minimized and those responsible for any use of nuclear weapons will be identifiable.

5. It should create the conditions in which nuclear weapons can by common consent (if this is forthcoming) be kept out of civil war in a nuclear power.

6. It should make possible so clear and detailed a knowledge of all the elements of power that miscalculation is made less likely.

7. The context it creates should offer a sufficient assurance to small powers in the event of aggression to prevent the growth of large armed forces in poor countries.

8. It should lead eventually to a structure for the peaceful

settlement of disputes through providing the context in which international law and custom can evolve.

9. It should preserve political variety with all the advantages of a plural world.

10. It should be capable of absorbing the attacks of adventurers whose object is to break down the working of the authority itself.

Success in the reform of power therefore depends more on skill in developing the necessary institutions than on anything else. If those institutions gain trust and respect from successful and reasonably impartial operation, they will more easily achieve and maintain the minimum consensus. If they are masters of changing technology, they will be able to adapt those areas of security which are being managed internationally to new facts. Gradually they might come to undertake the bulk of the responsibility for maintaining the international order and gain the trust of governments. States might cease to perceive the insecurity which is the basis of their heavy and burdensome defence efforts. If that were to happen the most effective disarmers, national finance ministers, would become irresistible. If a sense of security can be achieved it can be expected to disarm most states as effectively as insecurity has armed them in our time.

5

THE ACHIEVEMENT OF
COGNISANCE

IT has been argued that the formation of a conscious international security system in the presence of modern military technology requires the development of working institutions. It is obvious that they would have to grow from modest beginnings; and that their growth would depend on their proved ability to serve the cause of security. As with most domestic political institutions and the most advanced international ones, they will need both political and professional arms. Success in creating these, in keeping them relevant, and in making them effective could be the key to the peace.

If this line of argument is accepted, the immediate problem is to find the right way to begin such institutions. Their development is an end in itself but it cannot easily be pursued as such. The men and procedures needed can only be found in real efforts to solve genuine problems. Evident results are the best guarantee that governments will increase the resources and efforts they put into international security institutions and that they will trust them to take on increasing responsibilities. The best way to get such results is to undertake what can be achieved. Any security institution—the U.N. in the present world, for example—is likely to have exceptionally complex and difficult situations thrust on it by governments which hope that they can get the results which favour their interests and simultaneously avoid involvement. Those concerned with the reform of power and so with the strength and health of international security institutions should be eager to find those areas of service which have a good possibility of yielding real results.

An excellent first objective, and one that is fundamental to all longer term objectives, is to gain knowledge and understanding of the armed forces of the states of the world and the security policies these have been designed to serve. Most disarmament proposals purport to favour arrangements that will alter the shape and character of the weapons and formations which are capable of waging war. But if (as is argued here) it is unrealistic and undesirable to try to legislate against the right of individual or collective armament for states, it is nevertheless possible to argue that all power in the world is a legitimate subject of interest to the world as a whole. Weapons of mass destruction are properly and even inevitably objects of interest to all within range. Many of the conventional weapons in the armed forces of the world are of equally intense interest to others. An international security system must be founded on an international security dialogue; and that dialogue must concern itself first and foremost with what exists, how it might be used, and what is threatening the existing elements of order in the world.

A dialogue of this kind makes demands for the sort of structure that an effective international security system should eventually require. If governments could agree that their armed forces were a proper subject of international study and comment, both the professional and the political arms of an international institution could be developed with this as a central objective. Serving this activity and producing the basic elements for this debate would be a natural beginning for a professional staff organization. Governments would evolve their conscious international security policies in relation to real armed forces and not imaginary disarmed worlds. They would begin the task of explaining their own forces and policy in the face of hostile criticism. The underlying criteria of such a debate would be world security. The simple aim of knowledge could thus provide the basis for a valuable institutional development.

This evolution could also bring real security results. The absence of knowledge is a potent source of insecurity in certain circumstances. The failure to understand the nature and working of the present system can undermine the system itself; and the efforts which have been made to see that it is comprehended have greatly increased its strength. N.A.T.O.

experience is most instructive in this regard. This exceptionally advanced alliance structure has had to solve one of the basic problems of the present world order: the problem of guarantees. It has sought to bring the power of the United States into the calculations of both the Soviet Union and the countries of western Europe while at the same time uniting the main western European powers into a single security system. While N.A.T.O. has, of course, played a major part in organizing actual armed formations and developing a common strategy for war—a task not contemplated in the preliminary stages of international security organization—the conveyance of guarantees has been very important and may prove in retrospect to have been more fundamental to N.A.T.O.'s life.

The efforts to solve guarantee problems over the years are well known to students of European security problems. Although American, British, French, Belgian and Canadian troops have been based in Germany as a direct consequence of the Second World War and the occupation régime which followed it, their function as a means of committing the whole power of these states to the European *status quo* has always been important. Many other means to this objective have also been tried. For example, the addition of a great number of tactical nuclear explosives (more than 7000 warheads is the figure commonly quoted officially) to central European defence has been justified less as a means of fighting a battle than of showing determination and commitment to the use of nuclear weapons in the face of a successful Warsaw Pact attack. Great political energy was expended by the State Department, the Foreign Office and the West German government on the State Department's plan for a multilateral force (M.L.F.) of ship-borne Polaris missiles to be bought jointly and operated collectively with the primary object of reinforcing the commitment to strategic nuclear warfare in an equally dramatic way. These efforts were designed primarily to show that something existed rather than to achieve the thing itself.*

* The same rules seem to apply to crisis bargaining with opponents. The N.A.T.O. reinforcement of Berlin in the tense situation of 1961 was not designed primarily to defend West Berlin but to show that

A simpler exercise in cognisance at a powerful and expert level has emerged at a comparatively late stage in N.A.T.O.'s experience; and the evidence is accumulating that this is one of the most productive of the alliance's experiments. Mainly under the influence of Robert McNamara, and in the context of the U.S. abandonment of the M.L.F. project, a N.A.T.O. committee was established in 1965 under the name of the Nuclear Planning Group (N.P.G.). This body has since met twice a year at defence minister level and regularly at the level of permanent representatives to N.A.T.O.

Supported by a more professional Nuclear Defence Affairs Committee, the Nuclear Planning Group has achieved a particularly profound form of cognisance. Although the forces being discussed are mainly American, and the United States has no intention of giving any real control of them to others, the British and West German defence ministers (in particular) have joined in common discussion of when and how these forces might be used. This activity is, of course, justified by the fact that the forces are recognized to be part of a joint response and that America's N.A.T.O. allies have a fundamental interest in what the United States might do in a crisis. The Americans are prepared to let others share in their planning, secure in the knowledge that they have not alienated ultimate control over their forces and that they are still free to act as they choose in war. A political reality has, however, been superimposed on this basic technical independence. A contradiction is there only if control is thought to be the essential issue. In reality, the control issue is a secondary one on which a cautious government will want to reserve its rights as insurance against the unknown while pursuing its real alliance interests.

No doubt the central accomplishment of the N.P.G. and of the other N.A.T.O. efforts to achieve cognisance will be to

---

certain security realities—in this case, a readiness to face war—did in fact exist. The contemporary techniques of confrontation, unlike those of alliance and concert, are not, however, obviously relevant to the character of international security institutions.

reinforce the capacity of the N.A.T.O. group to fight a war together. It is in this sense an orthodox extension of the common commands which were established during the Korean War to defend western Europe from Soviet attack: and to this extent it teaches few lessons for broader international security purposes. But its genesis came in a very different era from the common commands and it may have become important in a way that was not anticipated. Apart altogether from the N.A.T.O.–Warsaw Pact confrontation, the N.P.G. studies and dialogue have served certain subjective realities in the thinking of governments. These realities are basic to their sense of security and so to their attitude to the international order. The new N.A.T.O. committees did not produce any new forces but they spread the conscious security benefits of what already existed to a group of countries. The Americans have found in N.A.T.O. that to give the West Germans and others true security it was necessary to plan jointly, not just to create a structure which made sense militarily to the United States. As a matter of objective fact, it is almost certainly true that on the basis of American and other power there is a North Atlantic security system and that this would work effectively in any foreseeable crisis. Those concerned with these matters in the U.S. believe this and so do their traditional confidants in the British Government.* But the objective fact achieves only some security objectives if it is not conveyed in a convincing form to those who are being asked to base their security on it.

The broader lessons of this for international security deserve exploration. Clearly, what has been needed to show the existence of a large-scale and ambitious western system in confrontation with the Warsaw Pact powers has been very different from what might be required on a global scale. But the central part which access to information and policy must play in any collective arrangements is indicated by the N.A.T.O. experience.

These considerations have an effect far beyond the world of

* Incidentally, reinforced by officers attached throughout every significant establishment in the U.S. armed forces, constituting what must surely be the most advanced system of cognisance ever created.

N.A.T.O. and the East–West confrontation. Many nations without major allies plan their armed forces and their security policy on the assumption that they live in some kind of world order. It is important for them and for the world as a whole that they should not become convinced that international society is in a Hobbesian state of nature in which every state is potentially an armed enemy of every other state. A growing sense of insecurity—quite probably in the presence of a modest but undefined system of international guarantees—will lead to greatly increased defence expenditure, particularly in the poor countries. This will obviously affect their economic development and, by shifting resources and power to the armed forces, their political character.

How much these risks would be avoided—how much, that is, there would be an increased sense of security—by the operation of an international system aimed at cognisance could easily be exaggerated. The effect might well be negligible. If, however, the major powers recognized that giving a sense of security was a central objective (as the Americans do with N.A.T.O.), institutions of this kind would help to achieve the objective.

This modest but very real objective rests on the premise that much security begins with knowledge. Where there is ignorance it is difficult to avoid fear and so insecurity. Those who want to convey security to others will make sure that they are informed. The primitive Soviet fear of western spying should not blind them to the fact that their own security has been increased by the relaxation in the West which has followed the development of more reliable ways of observing the Soviet armed forces. This would not be true, of course, if the Soviet Union were planning an attack on the West. In that case, good western intelligence would have done serious and perhaps fatal damage to the Soviet Union. But where a country is pursuing a defensive policy, and where it is offering guarantees (in the sense that it will not stand idle if another is attacked), means must be found to transmit evidence of these policies convincingly if the full benefits are to be achieved.

The international political debate about the armed forces and security policy of a particular country can lead in one of two directions. Either its military activities will gain general recognition as reasonable and acceptable; or they will be regarded as aggressive or unreasonable by some sector of international opinion. To the extent that they are the object of hostility, this fact could influence national defence policy. It is, of course, foolish to imagine that the views of others are going to influence any power which believes it has real security problems. But governments are commonly influenced by the need to account for their actions, even when those to whom they must account have no immediate sanction against them. Politicians prefer to have acceptable public positions and to head off critics well in advance. In parliamentary systems, civil servants are aware of the power of the still-unasked Parliamentary Question. In a Congressional system, the executive knows that it must have a reasonable story to put before Congressional committees. A good analogy is once more offered by the North Atlantic Treaty Organization. The N.A.T.O. Annual Review procedure subjects the forces and actions of the member countries to detailed scrutiny and obliges governments to account for their defence policy.

Many N.A.T.O. countries have mastered the problem of standing up to the annual attacks of the experienced N.A.T.O. officials who conduct the Review. But this has forced them to make a clear-cut policy decision to resist, which it would have been more convenient to avoid. The British Government, for example, is annually taken to task for not having its N.A.T.O.-assigned forces equipped as the N.A.T.O. planners believe they ought to be. Detailed and elaborate explanations are given, many of them the specious arguments of civil servants obliged to justify a policy out of its real context. But British forces outside the N.A.T.O. area can become run down or ill-equipped without anyone having to formulate any arguments about them. It is that much easier to do. An annual review procedure of this kind involves a peculiarly effective and intimate form of cognisance. It promises those who meet its canons an easy life and political convenience; and it threatens those who defy it with a context which is embarrassing and inconvenient.

The N.A.T.O. Annual Review is a highly classified exercise carried out by men with virtually complete access to all the facts. It is therefore a form of cognisance which would take a long time to achieve in international institutions, but it illustrates most usefully an elemental point about cognisance: namely, that a good deal of influence can be achieved over defence policy without having any control over it. In N.A.T.O. all governments retain complete independence to do what they please. But each member has chosen to make the N.A.T.O. arrangements a part of its security policy: and it voluntarily submits itself and its achievements to the criticism and assessment of those who are formally responsible to the alliance community as a whole. The criteria used in such a review procedure are, of course, of the first importance; and in N.A.T.O. they are based on the fairly simple proposition that what the alliance needs is the greatest possible power to resist Soviet invasion or attack. The criteria in a more general international effort would be more complex. They would be the interest of world security as a whole, and it is in this language that debate and analysis would be conducted.

The working of institutions designed for this purpose raises certain difficult questions. Can international security be divorced from the political hostilities of international life to the point where useful results can be anticipated? Can a country like the Soviet Union be expected to do anything but attack the entire security policy of, say, the Federal Republic of Germany or even the United States? Cannot the same thing be expected from Pakistan about India or Israel about the Arab countries? Would not any attempt to bring national security policies under international examination lead to greater opportunities for irresponsible political abuse?

The answer to this line of argument must be that in the first instance a system of cognisance would almost certainly lead to extreme political positions being taken on all sides of the political and military confrontations of the world. But even the act of asserting these positions would be of potential value to world security. The Russian who makes accusations against the Germans or Americans must recognize that the Germans and Americans are going to reply. Each will build up a position that will explain and justify his own policy. Each will be particularly ready to attack those elements in the rival's position which are likely to be difficult to explain away. This will be particularly true as the years pass and there is a better understanding of the issues. The very act of accusation or even political abuse will attract attention. People will inevitably be far more interested in what rivals like Pakistan and India are doing in Kashmir than in the affairs of two non-rivals. While rivals cannot be expected to feel deep sympathy for one another's security arrangements, they are likely over a period of time to find that it is most productive to subject the rival to criticism at the points where the threat to general security is most evident. This could influence his policy in important and constructive directions.

In whatever way this cognisance is achieved, it will inevitably be a political enterprise, with many of the disagreeable characteristics of working political institutions—bargains, double-dealing, deception and resentment. But these are accepted as part of the life of even the finest national constitutions. Although the idea of international institutions is still radiant with the goodness of those who have believed in them over the years, they will be frankly and grossly political when they come. This is already true of the United Nations' political organs or the bargaining in, for example, the G.A.T.T. Political idealism will have to find a new object on which to project its dreams: and it is to be hoped that there will be many patient idealists who will realize how much is at stake in making what international institutions there are do the tasks within their grasp as well as possible. Idealists of a gradualist frame of mind can also console themselves with the capacity of human institutions for growth and improvement when only such institutions can provide a needed authority and services.

These are the purposes of cognisance. It involves no transfer of control over any aspect of defence or security policy. It merely means that some sort of international institution makes all security policy its province and presumes to investigate the power that exists and the way it might be used.

Whether these purposes have any chance of being achieved depends on the techniques adopted and ultimately on how the institutions are worked. They must operate in such a way that it remains a basic national interest of all or nearly all of the decisive countries to participate in them and to give them at least the minimum co-operation needed.

The achievement of something of this kind demands both political institutions and skilled professionals. In this as in most other aspects of the reform of power the professionals are the most important part of the operation. It is they who can develop and maintain the common security interest below the level of active political dispute. Nevertheless, they must be the servants of an appropriate political structure and that structure is the obvious place in which to initiate an informed security dialogue. The claims of the United Nations to this role are obvious; and the Security Council exists nominally for the purpose. New institutions designed to avoid the particular political legacy of U.N. institutions can always take place on some linked basis. The Conference of the Committee on Disarmament (C.C.D.) is already in this position and the possibilities of development in the Geneva arrangements should not be overlooked. This distinguished body of representatives from most of the main powers—France (by abstention), China and Germany unfortunately excepted—debates at length its own version of the great problems of world security. The difficulty with the conference is that its participants have no particular knowledge either of security problems or of security policy in the main powers. Unfortunately they have had no incentive to gain such knowledge because the language of their debates is disarmament rather than security. Apart from the three main powers missing from its debates, it is also missing certain other important states such as Israel, Australia and South Africa. But these defects could easily be remedied. If the C.C.D. could be turned into the Defence Committee of the United Nations—hearing evidence, drawing up assessments, investigating, assessing the implications of the forces that exist and those that might exist—it could become a powerful force for cognisance. It could also gradually create the intellectual basis for a consensus over security policy, or at least over many elements of it.

No doubt a committee with these objectives would feel the need to equip itself with a professional staff. Certain national delegations would find it necessary to give themselves strong military backing, both to defend national policies and to discomfit adversaries. They would also be eager to gain acceptance for those elements of their policy which they considered important. The price of membership—indeed, a proper price for membership of the U.N. itself—should be an undertaking to give evidence about national defence policy in good faith, within the bounds of military security. Deceiving a committee of this kind would have the inconvenient consequence that the deceptions would be there on the record at a later date when the facts had become known. Depending on its rules and procedures, such a committee would no doubt be the arena for debate among rivals in periods of tension and confrontation. Though much of this would be unproductive, the effect on national policy of having to justify what is done and what is claimed before such a forum might well be useful. But for the great majority of routine peacetime military activity it would be extremely valuable to have national military establishments accept these techniques as normal. The existence of a world defence committee to which senior responsible men were obliged to report would help to break down the self-sufficient independence of defence departments operating on non-political assumptions and sealing themselves off from the international context of national policy.

The problem of finding the professionals could be solved in many different ways and would clearly depend on the character and skill of the top men. Security policy is highly technical and very specialized. Anyone who is to intervene in it must be professionally advised by a scientific, political-military and eventually military staff structure of as high a quality as possible.* In this regard attention should be given

* The best example of such a corps of men in an international context is probably the International Bank for Reconstruction and Development (the World Bank), which is the agent of the rich western powers

to the Military Staff Committee of the United Nations, which has achieved the remarkable feat of existing for more than a quarter of a century without doing anything. Here surely is evidence of the abiding faith of the group which founded the United Nations in the common security policy which they have been unable to discern.

The duty of the Military Staff Committee is outlined in Article 47 of the U.N. Charter: "To advise and assist the Security Council on all questions relating to the Security Council's military requirements for the maintenance of international peace and security, the employment and command of forces placed at its disposal, the regulation of armaments, and possible disarmament." The Committee is responsible "under the Security Council for the strategic direction of any armed forces placed at the disposal of the Security Council". While this committee, like the C.C.D., has the distinct advantage that it exists, it belongs to another period of defence policy. When it was created, the professional servants of security policy were military men. It is only during the intervening years that the planners and scientists followed by political-military officials have come into the defence field in an important way along with those whose training was more specifically based on the fighting arms. If the Military Staff Committee was to undertake the tasks that now face international security, it would have to develop very rapidly into something much broader in character than a group of high-ranking officers appointed to take responsibility for the operational direction of armed forces.

However the professional organization was constituted, it could properly begin its active life by laying the basis of common understanding of certain international security

---

in development and which has steadily built up a brilliant staff. An international security organization working in the minefield of East–West relations (among others) could not enjoy the freedom or the backing which made such a group possible. But if there is a point which is vital to success, and so to the achievement of growing international security, it is the quality of such a service.

questions. An obvious task, once performed by agencies of the League of Nations, is the publication of the basic known facts about the armed forces of the world in an authoritative form.* This is now being attempted under unofficial western auspices in *The Military Balance*, published annually by the Institute for Strategic Studies, London; and under unofficial neutral auspices in the *SIPRI Yearbook of World Armaments and Disarmament*, published annually by the Stockholm International Peace Research Institute.

Many detailed studies could usefully be done. This process has already begun under the authority of the Secretary-General of the United Nations through the Department of Political and Security Council Affairs. An excellent example is the report entitled *Chemical and Biological Weapons and the Effects of Their Use*, which was submitted to U Thant on 30 June 1969. The means by which this came to be written illustrate how a security organization might approach this aspect of its work. First, the annual report of the Eighteen Nation Disarmament Conference (as the C.C.D. was then called) recommended in 1969 that such a study should be done. The Secretary-General then put the proposal in his annual report and the General Assembly asked him† to prepare a report in co-operation with qualified experts. This he did, with one of his own men, Mr. William Epstein, as Chairman and a committee composed of senior officials (usually chief government scientists or the leading national expert on these weapons) from the United States, the Soviet Union, Britain, France, Japan, India, Canada, Sweden, Hungary, the Netherlands, Czechoslovakia, Mexico, Ethiopia and Poland. The resulting report quickly became a standard work in the field. It was identified officially with certain policy proposals by a Foreword signed by the Secretary-General and so produced outside the consensus needed for the report itself. In this, U Thant specifically opposed official western policy by calling for an end to the stockpiling of

* This idea was officially put forward by U Thant in a statement made before a conference on "The Politics of Disarmament" at the United Nations headquarters on 22 May 1970.

† General Assembly Resolution 2454A (XXIII).

chemical weapons (and "their effective elimination from the arsenal of weapons") as well as biological weapons. A case could be made for and against his decision to take this stand, which was disliked and resented by (among others) the United States and United Kingdom governments. It is certainly reasonable to assume that the higher authorities of an international security institution would have a much more subtle and realistic grasp of the security policies of member countries than is possible for a Secretary-General whose training and preoccupations are in other fields and who lacks a professional staff in these matters.

A remarkable international analogy for the kind of studies that might be contemplated is given by the publication programme of the O.E.C.D. These studies owe a great deal to the fact that the theoretical study of economics has become an independent discipline with an international language. Strategic studies are far behind but the analogy with economics exists, and governments and scholars are both coming to understand that what the Americans call the political-military is as real and as important a discipline as what English economists long ago entitled political economy.

The 22 countries of the O.E.C.D. describe themselves as partners in a permanent co-operation designed to harmonize national policies, as:

"1. An instrument for making available all knowledge relevant to the formulation of rational policy in every major field of economic activity.

"2. A forum, meeting the year round, in which such policies may be worked out in the light of shared ideas and experiences."

Its approach to the economic policies of its members (who, of course, remain entirely independent) is officially described as follows: "One of the most effective working methods, inherited from O.E.E.C., is the confrontation exercise in which the policies of each member country in turn are critically examined by all the other members in a frank discussion leading to the publication of both factual findings and policy recommendations. This co-operation has helped not only to prevent the recurrence of the serious economic crisis the world knew before the war but also to enable the various countries to embark together with greater confidence upon constructive, if sometimes difficult, policies." The relevance of such wording to international security is obvious.

The first major O.E.C.D. publication category is Economics. Economic policy lies at the heart of the organization's activity and the O.E.C.D. Economic Policy Committee brings together the main officials from participating countries two or three times a year. Great power and influence attaches to the three working parties of this committee, dealing respectively with balance of payments, economic growth policies and cost and price stability. The annual surveys of individual countries which O.E.C.D. publishes are the product of the Economic and Development Review Committee, which employs the confrontation method. The technique for carrying out an agreed policy in a complex field is demonstrated by O.E.C.D.'s work in, for example, the liberalization of capital movements and invisible operations. Codes have been drawn up in which member countries assume specific obligations. The Committee for Invisible Transactions then watches over the implementation of these codes. The relevance of such techniques to international security is also obvious.

As with the United Nations itself, it would seem reasonable to have a professional head of an international security institution who could speak out in his own name. He would require a high reputation and considerable political skill of the type made familiar by joint allied military commanders. Political realism, the essential quality, would obviously keep the staffs out of areas in which no consensus was likely, at least in the early years of its work. The organization would have to persuade governments that it existed to help to solve their security problems, not to destroy their security arrangements. To most governments, some of the best evidence for this would be the kind of men they themselves were able to send to serve in the organization and the results they were able to achieve. If the hypothesis of this study is correct—namely, that there is a clear and developing area of common security interest—a body of this kind should be able to serve the welfare of most governments. As for the men themselves, all the evidence of international military staffs is that military men in particular adapt quickly and easily to the new environment and to new, if temporary, loyalties—provided they know that this is what is expected of them by their government.

If politically and professionally an increasing cognisance over force is achieved, great benefits should show themselves over the years in two ways. The first is that professional attention to common security should create a political context in which informal arms control measures can be adopted without too much fanfare. The second is that the medium and small powers could be persuaded that they live in a reasonable structure of world security and not in an international state of nature: and that it is therefore not necessary for them to spend heavily on weapons in order to ensure that their successors will have some means of defying the law of the jungle. This psychological issue is probably basic to the solution of the problem of nuclear proliferation. A decision now not to produce nuclear weapons affects what the country will have in two decades. Many countries want to avoid this decision and, above all, to avoid the expenditure involved in a full-scale programme. But can they conscientiously abjure the decisive weapons which are being constructed in such numbers by the major powers? Is anyone responsible for their security but themselves? More will be required before most middle powers share the views of a secure country like Canada that these questions no longer pose dilemmas. But the sense that they are in a growing system (the sense that most N.A.T.O. powers were given in the 1950s) would powerfully reinforce the financial—and occasionally moral and political—reluctance of many countries. What is true of nuclear weapons will also be true of other forms of military power. A system of cognisance will show that some structure of guarantees probably exists, at least for most purposes. It could give some tangible substance to the optimistic assumptions which still underlie the military policies of most governments.

Its main achievement, however, would be to bring

conscious international security to life and to create a conscious relationship with the national security policies of states. The institutions and men that could do this would be well placed to carry the reform forward if an effective concert of the powers wanted to see this happen.

6

AN EXPANDING
SECURITY SYSTEM

COGNISANCE is a good broad starting-point for international
security institutions. It involves governments in a genuine
commitment and yet it poses no threat to their security. It
gives the world order a chance to become self-conscious, at
least to some extent; and it allows international servants to
show governments that they can be trusted.

Clearly, however, the institutions must get to work at an
early date on the management and control of substantive
security issues. International security cannot be confined indefinitely to collective study and debate. It must show
its ability to take responsibility and to deal with real
problems. There are already a number of matters which are
badly in need of management at the world level and which
are unlikely to be dealt with at any other level. Some of these
have been generally recognized: and the successful operation
of an international structure would soon reveal more.

There can be no illusions about the immense complexity of
the task, even in the preliminary stages. Disarmament
thinking in the past has recognized the difficulty of achieving
political agreement, but has rejoiced in the apparent simplicity of the disarmament process itself once the political
winds turned favourable. An international system of the kind
being considered here can only expect quite extraordinarily
difficult tasks in a demanding political environment. Governments may want the larger objectives but they will resist the
necessary commitments. They will also be persuaded by their
own interest groups to fight specific measures which affect
them. As in many other international institutions, security
institutions will stand or fall by their ability to pick the right
issues and handle the significant government authorities with

discretion and skill. The right issues are clearly those in which the general security interest is greatest and most evident, and the consequences of drift most serious. The lines of advance at any given time must be a matter of debate and speculation and the result of an effective dialogue among governments; but all this is the business of turning a theoretical (if evident) world interest into a political reality.

I *Strategic nuclear weapons*

One of the obvious places to start is in the range of problems raised by strategic nuclear weapons. Since the invention and use of these explosives, there has been a strong and virtually universal sense that they constituted a major problem for the world as a whole. Agreements have been reached covering important aspects of their testing, deployment and proliferation; alliance structures for common targeting and planning have been built up; and the United States and the Soviet Union, the two great strategic nuclear powers, have embarked on a serious effort to find ways to achieve mutual limitation in these arms.

This Soviet–American dialogue had its origins well before the S.A.L.T. talks and has exhibited some of the characteristics of a permanently operating factor in international life. The evidence suggests that an international security organization should take up the problem of strategic nuclear weapons deployment early and vigorously. Although the secondary nuclear powers have shown little desire to expose their nuclear efforts to public gaze, the Americans have developed a strong desire to influence the policies of others and the Soviet Union has at least seen the tactical advantages which might be derived from the American readiness to talk.

Some notion of international security has played a real and conscious part in America's nuclear defence planning for many years. This in itself was tending towards international arrangements, or at least an effective dialogue. The administration decided in 1968, however, that there were specific possibilities of weapons development in the Soviet Union that could be dangerous for the American strategic weapons force; and that some incentive should be given to the Soviet Government to design its forces in what the Americans would regard as the common interest. It was thus the United States, responding to the Soviet weapons programme, which sponsored the idea of Strategic Arms Limitation Talks which began in Helsinki in 1969 after some delays. The view of the Kennedy and Johnson administrations on this matter was summed up in remarkably strong language by Mr. McGeorge Bundy, who had been special assistant to both Presidents for National Security Affairs:*

The search for a grip on the race in nuclear arms is now an imperative *which is very nearly absolute*. The talks which have now begun will not be easy or short, for the questions presented are much more difficult than those we have resolved in earlier nuclear agreements; but their success matters enormously to us all. The multiplication of nuclear warheads, along with the constantly accelerating technology of their delivery and their defence, offers a prospect of such danger and diversion of effort that it is way past time for sensible states to put a stop to it.

President Nixon's first major foreign and defence policy review† took up the theme of Soviet advance in strategic nuclear weapons systems. Both their numbers and their quality, he said, were improving. By the end of 1970 the Soviet Union would have 1290 intercontinental missiles to 1054 in the U.S. and 300 submarine-launched ballistic missiles to 656 in the U.S. In contrast, the American predominance in the two categories together in mid-1965 had been 1398 to 331.

President Nixon formulated four questions: "Will the Soviets continue to expand their strategic forces? What will be their configuration? What understanding might we reach on strategic arms limitations? What weapons systems might be covered by agreements?" Decisions on shaping the future

* *The Round Table*, No. 237, January 1970, p. 7. The italics have been inserted.

† "United States Foreign Policy for the 1970s: A New Strategy for Peace", a report to the Congress, 18 February 1970.

strategic posture were perhaps, he wrote, the most complex and fateful they faced.

The answers to these questions will largely determine whether we will be forced into increased deployments to offset the Soviet threat to the sufficiency of our deterrent, or whether we and the Soviet Union can together move from an era of confrontation to one of negotiation; whether jointly we can pursue responsible, non-provocative strategic arms policies based on sufficiency as a mutually shared goal or whether there will be another round of the arms race.

This statement sums up the central theme of the first year of the Nixon Administration, itself the established policy of the preceding Johnson Administration. It is worth noting that the nearly absolute imperative of which Mr. Bundy wrote was shown beyond doubt by the response of the United States to the Soviet invasion of Czechoslovakia in August 1968. At that time, the preparations for strategic arms talks were well advanced and the President was speculating about the possibility of launching the talks at a prestigious heads of government conference. Then came the Czech events—to western eyes an outrage of very considerable proportions. In another age they would have led to a rapid disintegration of relations. They did in fact delay the opening of the strategic talks but this was no more than a concession to public opinion and an international sense of decency. When an appropriate period had elapsed things went on as before. Neither the President nor his principal advisers saw any essential connection between Czechoslovakia and S.A.L.T. The strategic realities were unchanged and it was these which dominated the thinking of both U.S. administrations. Clearly, the U.S. authorities believed that permanent factors were operating: and these were to a large extent independent of the political context.

There is no particular reason to think that U.S. and Soviet thinking in these matters has run in parallel. As usual, the United States has conducted much of its debate in public; and though there are different layers to the argument the main lines of reasoning are comparatively easy to follow. In the

Soviet case, it would be presumptuous to conclude that the predominant political forces have yet come to accept the desirability of pursuing strategic arms policies "jointly" (the word used by President Nixon). The American debate alone, however, is adequate to show the extent to which in strategic nuclear arms there are powerful secular pressures towards international security.

The working out of these pressures and the establishment of a common U.S.–Soviet approach is in itself a matter of great complexity. Its broadening to include an effective consensus of other powers and the discovery of its application to Britain, France, Japan and West Germany (not to mention China) will be a laborious affair; and it may well in itself be a source of strain in the international order. Nevertheless the thing must be done. The present system cannot be expected to maintain its strength without a determination by all concerned not to destroy the essential elements in it which are in the care of rival powers. The search for an international policy must therefore start with an examination of the thinking of the United States and the Soviet Union about their own heavy nuclear forces.

The American approach has certain visible elements to it.* For many years, the United States has had an assured capacity to destroy the cities of the Soviet Union. She has also had a large force able to strike a great range of Soviet military targets. This force was particularly impressive on the assumption that the U.S. herself had not been subject to heavy nuclear attack; but it remained impressive even assuming such an attack.

In the late 1960s the Americans experienced a sense that their effectiveness against the Soviet strategic bomber and missile forces was gradually ebbing away. The pressures on the target planners grew and so, proportionately, did their requests for forces. Where previously there had been a relatively short target list of bomber bases and soft missile sites, the evolution of the Soviet armed forces caused a requirement for increasing numbers of attacking warheads. Hardened Soviet missiles required more and larger blasts to be reasonably

* See Chapter 1.

certain of their destruction; radars of importance to both aircraft and missile defences were multiplying very rapidly; a substantial number of naval targets emerged; and the number of Soviet missiles themselves was growing constantly.

In spite of the many other explanations which have been given—a desire for a true first strike capability, the unstoppable logic of arms development, the need to remain effective against the growing Soviet ballistic missile defences—it is probable that the strong technical and financial backing for the American M.I.R.V. programme came primarily from this source.* The cost of producing more Minuteman or

* The official public position of the U.S. Administration is that the M.I.R.V. programmes were forced on the U.S. by the Soviet missile defences of cities. The most systematic statement of this position was made by Dr. John S. Foster, Director of Defense Research and Engineering: "For adequate assurance that our forces will be able to deter and attack, our weapons must be able to survive an attack on their bases and must be able to penetrate reliably any defenses arrayed against them. The second requirement, the penetration of ballistic missile defences at Soviet cities, has determined our deployment of these MIRVed systems. . . . Since the early 1960s, when it became evident that the Soviets were developing ABM technology and appeared to be fielding an ABM, we have deployed both types of penetration aids on our operational missiles. Multiple reentry vehicles are deployed on the existing Polaris A-3 missiles. However, both the Polaris multiples and our other early penetration aids were deployed in a way that placed them relatively close to one another when they arrived near the target.

"In 1964 we had indications that the Soviets were deploying a new type of ABM system when a new ABM interceptor was displayed in Moscow. This is the missile which has been called Galosh. It is a very large missile and must be assumed to have the capability of carrying a multiple-megaton warhead. This improved Soviet ABM warhead raised the possibility that one defensive explosive burst could destroy more than one threatening object. Also, the Soviets have deployed ABM radars and missiles in the Moscow area. And, potentially even more serious, they have deployed large numbers of another defensive system, the so-called Tallinn system, which could be converted into an effective ABM defense of Soviet urban-industrial areas.

"Soviet defense, in other words, could achieve the potential to intercept and destroy a significant percentage of the American deterrent missile warheads and therefore could threaten the credibility and effectiveness of our deterrent. We need a more reliable method of

Polaris to handle the growing lists was unacceptable. The M.I.R.V. offered a much cheaper way to achieve something like the same result.

There is no evidence, however, that the Americans believed that their first generation of M.I.R.V.s could return them to the position they had probably enjoyed in 1965: the situation, that is, in which a decision to embark on strategic nuclear war could be expected to result in the elimination of most long-range Soviet nuclear forces before they could be fired. The present weapons are not accurate enough.* A later generation of M.I.R.V.s with much higher accuracy can be anticipated and is being planned. But for the present the necessary navigational systems (and the redesigned re-entry vehicles to incorporate them) are still not fully developed.

* Congressional testimony on the Safeguard A.B.M. revealed that an average miss-distance of 440 yards or less was needed to give a warhead of several megatons a high probability of destroying a Minuteman silo. American M.I.R.V.s have much smaller warheads than this and would therefore need extreme accuracies. Of course, there are many military targets which are much less protected than a Minuteman silo and which U.S. M.I.R.V.s are designed to destroy.

---

delivering our deception devices and our warheads. We need to be able, essentially, to spread them out in space so that one Soviet defensive nuclear burst cannot destroy several American warheads or a whole cloud of decoys. We did not want to solve this problem by adding to the number of American offensive missile launchers. Increased numbers of missile launchers could, of course, ensure penetration of Soviet city defences. This solution to the problem, however, would carry an unacceptably high risk of stimulating the arms race, which we would like to avoid if at all possible.

"Instead, we turned to Minuteman and Polaris improvements that could give us individually directed MRVs, or MIRV. This technology will allow us to send the RVs either to a single target or to a number of targets. This is why we call them MIRV, multiple individually targeted re-entry vehicles. Technologies of this type had been considered since about 1960 for the purpose of increasing the target coverage of a single missile. However, the United States decision to deploy this technology was based primarily upon our requirement to penetrate Soviet defenses, not upon its multiple-target capability." Hearings before the Subcommittee on National Security Policy and Scientific Developments of the House Committee on Foreign Affairs, pages 242–3. Government Printing Office, Washington, 1969.

The best that the Americans can expect of their M.I.R.V.s is that by increasing sharply the numbers of explosives available the offensive forces and the target list will be kept in some kind of balance.

The emphasis on accuracy is to be found in the Congressional testimony on M.I.R.V.s by Dr. George B. Kistiakowsky, a scientist of great experience, who is always close to U.S. policy:*

A new element of nuclear peace instability may be introduced if a nation deploys MIRVs that have been made highly accurate and proven so by extensive testing. A nation having deployed these has the option, whether it plans to use it or not, for a far more effective first strike because each of its MIRV equipped missiles can destroy, on the average, more than one of its opponent's missile silos. At least its adversary must perceive that as a possibility. Therein, of course, is the essence of the destabilizing effect of highly accurate MIRVs. . . . A specific consequence in the foreseeable future of a deployment of highly reliable MIRVs by the Soviet Union is that the reliability of our Minuteman force as a deterrent will be greatly weakened.

Accuracy is as clearly stated but much less emphasized by Dr. Foster. In his testimony claiming that the U.S. M.I.R.V. force constituted no threat to the Soviet retaliatory forces, he carefully inserted the qualification about accuracy but did not emphasize it:†

By splitting up the payload of the Minuteman and Polaris boosters into several MIRVs, we necessarily lose a substantial portion of the total megatonnage of our deterrent missile forces and a substantial portion of the nuclear explosive power that can be delivered by each booster. The explosive yields in our MIRVs are small. . . . For defence penetration, our MIRV warheads must be numerous and thus small, so, *given approximately equal accuracy*, the multiple individually guided warheads will not add

* Hearings before the Subcommittee on National Security Policy and Scientific Developments of the House Committee on Foreign Affairs, p. 87. The statement was made on 15 July 1969.

† Ibid., p. 244. The italics have been added.

significantly over the single re-entry vehicle missile ability to destroy hardened Soviet weapons.

It seems true to say, therefore, that while the Americans have made some effort to keep their counterforce option they easily resigned themselves to its loss when it became clear that this was what was happening. In so far as the capacity to disarm the Russian missile force existed, the Americans always regarded it as a bonus which could not normally be expected. Their main concern was that the Soviet forces should never enjoy the advantage which their own forces had probably had but which they had neither claimed nor used (except in the sense that it made them extremely confident during what little bargaining there had been in the period).

The prospect of a Soviet force which could disarm the American retaliatory forces is not new to the American imagination. It has been seen* that this was a major theme in the U.S. debate in the 1950s. It has re-emerged strongly in the 1970s with the Administration attacks on the Soviet SS-9 programme and the growing concern with the numbers of offensive missiles in place or in construction in the Soviet Union. The totals of Soviet missiles, whatever they may have been from time to time, have had to be increased for future years by the rate of production the Soviets have shown they could achieve. Obviously, the force will not become infinitely large. Equally obviously, however, there is no point at which the Americans and their allies can feel free to assume that this will be the full complement. The basis for the fear about the SS-9 has been stated by Dr. Foster:†

Although we are not positive that the multiple warheads being tested on the Soviet SS-9 ICBM are designed for multiple hard-target destruction, we do know that the guidance and control system employed in the SS-9 tests has capabilities much greater than that required to implement a simple MRV. . . My own judgement in this matter is that the Soviet triplet probably is a MIRV and that it has little other function than the attack of

* See Chapter 2.

† Hearings of the National Security Policy Subcommittee of the House Foreign Affairs Committee, Washington, 5 August 1969, pp. 244–5.

large numbers of hard targets. . . . Now, the SS-9 carrying a large
warhead would have more than adequate capability against a
Minuteman silo, because the SS-9 carries a very large total payload and is rather accurate. When the Soviets split the SS-9 payload into three warheads, each one of these warheads would be
well into the megaton range and would still have adequate
capability against a single Minuteman silo. In this regard—
warhead size and capability for first strike—our MIRV and the
likely Soviet MIRV are not symmetrical. The capability and
the purpose of our MIRVs are against the Soviet defenses, and the
capability of their MIRVs appears to be against our Minuteman.
Of course, we cannot know their MIRVs' purpose. That is locked
in the minds of the men in the Kremlin.

The American administration has speculated openly about
its possible responses to this situation should agreed limitation
fail. They can superharden their bases, find new forms of
mobility, or construct active defences for their weapons. They
can also, of course, produce far more weapons. The two
responses getting most consideration at present are a larger
and longer-range missile-firing submarine and a Minuteman
fortress concept based on increasingly effective ballistic
missile defences.

Soviet policy is by no means as accessible as United States
policy: and clearly one of the first achievements of a strategic
arms dialogue—either in S.A.L.T. or in a broader and more
permanent international institution—must be to make Soviet
strategic thinking accessible to those who would like to see a
reform of power. Quite basic questions about Soviet policy
have never really been settled in the western debate. It can
be argued, for example, that the notion of an assured destruction capability is not integral to Soviet general war thinking,
which has retained the orthodox notion that victory can
only be achieved through defeat of the enemy on the ground
(and presumable occupation). For many years, it was even
arguable that the Soviet bomber and missile forces directed at
North America were designed to hit targets which were
directly related to the progress of a European land battle.
While major ports and other population centres might well

come into such a target system, the strikes would be launched in support of the land battle. However difficult to distinguish in practice, such a doctrine is a long way from Anglo-American notions of strategic war and assured destruction.

Whatever may have been true in earlier days, it now seems likely that the Soviet Union has coherent objectives that western thinking would regard as strategic and nuclear. There is also an obvious Soviet need to avoid a repetition of the kind of American disarming capability which seemed to exist in the 1960s. Whatever the purpose of Soviet long-range bomber and missile forces, it can be no part of the Soviet intention that they should be exposed to destruction in a surprise attack. As it became obvious to the Soviet high command that the notion of nuclear superiority was psychologically important to the American position in the world, there may well have been a conscious decision to challenge this and to achieve equality for its own sake. Some may have argued that a superiority which could be shown to have been politically useful to the United States could be equally useful to the Soviet Union.

Whatever the successful arguments, there can be little doubt that the Soviet Union has become deeply engaged in the development and maintenance of a large nuclear force with warheads far more powerful than those deployed by any other country. It is also clear that she has spent heavily on defences. While American deterrence doctrine led her to spend three times as much on offensive as defensive forces, the Soviet Union was for many years spending three times as much on defensive forces as on offensive forces. The early type of ballistic missile defence system—which under the name of Nike Zeus was strongly advocated by the Chiefs of Staff in the United States and constantly resisted by Presidents Eisenhower and Kennedy—was constructed in the Soviet Union. It is not surprising that a great power whose principal rival has embraced strategic bombardment as a primary war-winning weapon for 30 years should have invested heavily in defences against such strategic bombardment. Western analysis of these matters remains speculative and the conclusions are in dispute. To meet the Soviet security need it will be necessary to develop techniques by which those concerned with international security can comprehend the basic Soviet defence instinct. Any effort to find where the common interest lies will have to probe carefully into the true objectives of Soviet military policy. The matter cannot be prejudged in the West.

Even without any sure knowledge of Soviet objectives, there is a clear common interest in the avoidance of expansion on both sides based on the need for pessimistic technical assumptions. A period of rapid development on new weapons such as the M.I.R.V. and the A.B.M. is inevitably one of great uncertainty. When, however, this is combined with the varying ratios which these offensive and defensive weapons can have to each other; with the considerable technical uncertainties which surround such very advanced equipment; and with the completely unknowable environment of total nuclear war in which alone they would be used in any numbers, the range of possible decisions must become very wide. Even if both sides were to make identical assumptions but felt they must err on the side of caution, they would find themselves operating on a very different basis. Cautious planning by two rival governments therefore seems likely to leave both sides more insecure. The national and international security interests in a situation of this kind become virtually identical.

In these circumstances, it is clearly in the interest of each side to give the assurances which are necessary to prevent a dangerous reaction on the other side. This is, however, exceptionally difficult to accomplish. The transmission of allegedly secret information of a misleading character is a well-developed governmental technique in matters of major security interest. Great skill will be required to construct a system by which countries could obtain information on so reliable a basis that they would allow it to influence their planning in a conservative direction. Exchanges of men and access to testing and other information would have to go very far. Yet it is a mutual interest of a particularly dramatic kind. The depth and extent of the problem provide a common security institution with a unique opportunity to show that it can serve at the very heart of national security policy in the major nuclear powers. If it succeeded in penetrating secrecy to the point where it could give reliable assurances (or provide the framework in which the authorities could obtain them), it would have entered deeply into the world security order.

All serious disarmament and arms control proposals in the past have come up against difficult problems of verification, and an international security institution working with national security policies will not escape from these difficulties. The issue is not primarily one of penetrating the secrets of governments; it is of giving other governments an assurance that certain dangerous things, to which they would react, are not taking place. Here, once more, one can speculate about the possibility of an institutional development. World security is going to involve very great quantities of information, derived from many sources. One need only consider the problems being thrown up by the potential for chemical and biological weapons in drug companies or of plutonium diversion from reactors to see how deeply security policy is going to have to penetrate into every society in future. This combined with the enormous security advantages of assurances which can be trusted suggests that thought and study should be given to the creation of a professional mechanism serving an international institution. One is reminded of the parallel of the chartered accountant or certified accountant: a profession which deals constantly in confidential information of great commercial value and which exists purely because of its integrity. Other centuries seem to have been more able than our own to recognize a new kind of need and train a new type of man to handle it under the special circumstances imposed by the situation. It is not just the laws (in the traditional formulation of natural law) which derive from the nature of things. Political society in all its spheres must find the appropriate response to realities: and so to changing realities. A piece of international machinery which could achieve high standards of inspection while enjoying general confidence that it was no threat to secrets would be an immense accomplishment.

Like any institutional development, it would, of course, take time.

The immediate objective in strategic nuclear arms is to bring about restraint in those weapons programmes which are obviously worrying others. While this might be the reverse of what one might be expected to do in a cold war, it is a common thing in peacetime military conduct. It is obvious that the United States administration is very concerned about the rate of deployment of the Soviet SS-9 and SS-11 ballistic missiles. It is not so obvious what the Soviets dislike: though on western arguments they should be concerned about the size of the Minuteman force and the development of potentially accurate guidance systems for American multiple warheads. If they are concerned about their assured destruction capabilities, they must also be anxious about the advances in ballistic missile defence technology in the United States and the prospect that an effective system might be extended at some point to the cities.

The Soviet attitude to the Western notion of mutual deterrence is obviously central to the consideration of the future of strategic nuclear forces. To proceed on the basis that an assured destruction capability should be preserved is very different from an effort to secure each side from nuclear attack. However logical it may seem to the Americans and most of their allies, the notion of mutual deterrence is something of a strategic curiosity. It cannot be assumed that it makes as much sense in Moscow, with its historic memories, as it does in Washington or London, with their memories.

If mutual deterrence can be established as an objective, certain quite simple objectives flow from it. The ability to destroy strategic weapons—or at least those directed against cities and comparable targets—becomes undesirable while the ability to destroy cities is desirable. Defensive forces work the other way. City defences diminish stability while the defences of strategic weapons increase it. On these arguments, it is not difficult to show that the American strategic forces are large but tolerable; that an American city defence on a substantial scale or an accurate M.I.R.V. would be dangerous to Soviet security; that the Soviet strategic forces are large but tolerable; and that a great increase in high-yielding Soviet re-entry vehicles or a vast city defence would be dangerous to American security. While tolerant towards the *status quo*, these mutual deterrence arguments would certainly tend to reduce the very large numbers of strategic weapons maintained by the two major nuclear powers.

These objectives have, of course, been identified by the Americans in going into strategic arms limitation talks with the Soviet Union. It may be doubted, however, whether they can be achieved in a simple bilateral series of understandings. The subject matter is simple in principle but complex and ill-defined in practice. Real results, especially if they are to avoid the risks of a sense of betrayal, will require a continuing dialogue and expert attention. President Nixon has talked of proceeding "jointly". The implications of this may be more far-reaching than he has admitted.

Other powers have important interests in the matter. The N.A.T.O. countries and other American allies are obviously concerned about the effects of an agreement of this kind on their own security policy. Politically, they must ask whether the U.S. has not in a real sense entered into a general alliance with the Soviet Union with broad commitments. And militarily, they must ask whether the nuclear strategy on which to a greater or lesser extent they had relied might not be in jeopardy. In return, the Americans and Russians are likely to want to know what limits can be expected on the nuclear forces of others. As time goes on, they will want to engage in a comparable dialogue with them.

The short-term nuclear problem seems to be primarily, therefore, not to allow disintegration into a more dangerous condition and to develop an effective dialogue among the main powers. The two major powers, in particular, must come to believe that unrestricted nuclear weapons production, like mobilization in 1914, can be a dangerous thing and can no longer be thought the simple prerogative of a sovereign state. But both militarily and politically, the implications of this will inevitably widen. The security of submarine-based nuclear forces—now an important part of the American and Soviet strategic forces as well as the British and (in future) the

French—will raise important questions about anti-submarine forces. Certain types of detection will probably have to be restricted by agreement. The Soviet Union has already raised the question of the longer-range N.A.T.O. nuclear weapons in Europe as an element in any discussion of strategic arms limitation: and for this and other reasons any S.A.L.T.-type negotiation inevitably opens the broad issues of European security. A Soviet-American dialogue on strategic arms may be possible because the issue seems seductively mathematical and non-political. Once engaged, however, it is likely to make demands for decisions over a wide range of security policy. This could provide valuable energy for the complexities of more far-reaching reform.

The strange character of assured destruction (and the terrible weapons which support it) suggests that a longer term view of the place of strategic nuclear weapons is needed for any programme of reform. What is done beyond avoiding the worst dangers in armaments development will be influenced by the kind of organization which seems tolerable or even desirable over a substantial period of time. An attempt to assess this will be made in the next chapter.

II   *The control of nuclear materials*

Another major branch of security which demands action at a world level is summed up by the phrase nuclear proliferation. Here once more there has already been general acceptance of the need for common action, as represented by the non-proliferation treaty and the safeguards system. It seems clear, however, that these instruments are inadequate to what is expected of them; and that the barriers to the production of nuclear weapons by an increasing number of countries are steadily coming down. Plutonium production capacity is being built up in one country after another. This will lead to plutonium stockpiles; and even where reactors have not been operated so as to produce good weapons-grade plutonium the decision to do this can be taken at any time. Uranium enrichment facilities are some years behind: but the political inhibitions to building up stocks of partially enriched uranium* and to the sale of plants capable of enriching uranium have largely disappeared.

This urgent and serious situation has been allowed to develop because there has been no realistic machinery capable of engaging the problem. Faced with their own impotence, the major powers have taken consolation in their deterrents and persuaded themselves that if nuclear weapons are going to spread there is nothing they can do about it: and that in any case, with their nuclear forces, they will remain inviolate. Reassurance is offered by strategists in theories of deterrence; by lawyers in exposition of the safeguards system; by commercial men in the traditional liberal view that what is good for the economy is good for the peace; and by scientists in their view that whatever removes barriers to knowledge must serve peace and progress. None will stand scrutiny. The problem is real and growing; and it demands the kind of determined international action which the nineteenth century put into the posts and telegraph and the twentieth into building up an international system of civil aviation.

A system which can support the spread of reactors around the world must probably return to the basic objective of the Baruch Plan: the control of nuclear fuels. To avoid having the stockpiles come into the hands of one state after another, the most hopeful solution is that they should be internationally owned. It would clearly be expensive to create an agency which leased fuel instead of selling it and which took back irradiated fuel rods with appropriate credits for the plutonium they contained. But the expense would be investment expense: the money put into the development of banks of materials of this kind would be balanced against assets which (if the prices were appropriate) would equal the costs.

There would be great commercial advantages in such a system, particularly for small and poor countries. An international agency which owned great quantities of natural uranium, enriched uranium at various levels, plutonium and

* The Americans now offer five years' pre-stocking of enriched uranium fuel as a standard undertaking in contracts for American enriched uranium reactors.

other nuclear materials, and which made these available at satisfactory rates, would be a great source of commercial security to those who now feel they must place themselves in the hands of the major industrial powers in order to secure their future power resources. Countries are already accumulating stocks of plutonium and other materials at very great cost in order to be sure of their future commercial arrangements. The opportunity to rent what is needed and the assurance that in the foreseeable future anything that might be needed would be available would represent a great saving.

Nothing in such a system would prevent countries from embarking on a national nuclear weapons programme when they felt this was necessary. They would not be able to do this, however, with existing stockpiles. They could seize the fuel which at any given time might be in their reactors; but this would be a seizure of materials owned by others and would be a dangerously aggressive act. It is perhaps an exaggeration to say that it would be equivalent to seizing the warships (or missile-firing submarines) of another power when they were in your port; but it would have the same character, and international society would undoubtedly react severely.

Suggestions of this kind occasionally encounter the argument that the stockpiles must be somewhere and that thus they are open to seizure by the host country. This argument need not be taken seriously. First, the same considerations apply: West Germans or East Germans might perhaps like to possess nuclear weapons but neither would consider seizing the American or Russian ones on their territory.* Second, the agency would be able to create its stocks in places of its choice; and if it is impossible or invidious to select politically reliable hosts, there is always the fact that the major nuclear powers are satiated with their nuclear stocks and are too rich to be tempted to turn bank robber.

As part of a structure of this kind, it would be immensely

* It is worth noting that the very deep Soviet fear of German nuclear weapons does not extend in any significant way to the thousands of American nuclear weapons under German sovereign control. Ownership is basic.

advantageous if fuel processing plants were owned internationally. If the existing nuclear powers could be persuaded to adopt the traditional American disarmament proposal of the cut-off—that is, an end to the building up of nuclear stockpiles—all new production of plutonium could then pass under the surveillance of international authorities. If these authorities were undertaking responsibility for the supply of nuclear fuels, they would have a legitimate claim to own and operate the existing plutonium separation facilities in the nuclear powers, in Belgium, in India and in Japan. The growing number of these facilities (built with the co-operation and equipment of the major powers) can be traced in part to the desire to acquire options on national nuclear weapons.

A system which concentrated on fuels and fuel processing would also be attracted to uranium enrichment plants. As was argued in Chapter 1, this is the decisive technology; and if, as is widely hoped, the high-speed gas centrifuge process produces economical results and centrifuges become widely available, the barriers that keep many countries from thermonuclear weapons will be permanently dismantled. No issue needs to be grasped so urgently and so firmly by those who might accept responsibility for international security. In the context of a cut-off, uranium enrichment plants (like plutonium separation plants) would cease to have any military purposes anywhere. They could be devoted to the requirements of the world economy and run for the purpose of maintaining the desired stocks of the many varieties of nuclear fuel. It may be doubted whether there would be any need to place these facilities on the soil of countries which do not now possess them.

An international institution of this kind would be open to many criticisms: that it was a monopoly; that it was trying to preserve the advantages of a narrow group of states; that (*per contra*) it was removing facilities vital to national security in the U.S., Soviet Union, U.K., France, etc. and placing these in the hands of an incoherent international agency; that no one would build exceedingly expensive power plants and come to depend on them if the fuel was in the hands of a distant authority;* and so on. These objections can be applied in various ways to the International Air Transport Association and other bodies. In the nuclear field, they are obviously important. All that can be said is that they are not nearly so important as the development of a genuine international atomic energy system before nuclear facilities and materials have spread so widely that everything needed for nuclear weapons is available to many governments.

An attempt to organize the world nuclear industry on these principles would have security objectives and would reflect changing security needs. Obviously, one or more agencies would be needed to handle the complexities of the industrial side of the operation. Equally, the principles on which this was administered would have to be continuously influenced by security considerations, as a national atomic energy commission is influenced by the changing national security interest. The agencies of international security would need the intelligence and the technical skill to stay on top of the technology and to see that the international interest in non-proliferation was not undermined by commercial forces or by irresponsible efforts by the major powers to buy the support of small powers.

III   *The avoidance and handling of nuclear accidents*

Another early objective for international security institutions is to deal with the political and military problems raised by the possibility of an accidental use of nuclear weapons. Something of a caricature of what is nevertheless a real problem is to be found in the authoritative pages of Marshal Sokolovsky:†

"Due to the arms race, there is a serious danger that even a small error by state leaders could lead to a new war. Nuclear

---

* A country like South Africa, Israel or East Germany well might consider, with reason, that an international organization might be tempted to use its power over fuels for coercion. This is a real problem and can be resolved only by consistent fidelity to the basic rule that all peaceful requirements will be filled in all circumstances.

† *Military Strategy: Soviet Doctrine and Concepts*, op. cit., p. 183.

weapons can be launched not only on the command of a government but also at the discretion of individuals at the control panel. Careless operations of radar systems can cause an incorrect interpretation of instrument readings and this could lead to the beginning of military activities. Incorrect understanding of an order or the mental disorder in the case of an American pilot flying a bomber armed with nuclear warheads could cause the bombs to be dropped on the territory of another country. Faults in electronic equipment of combat nuclear-missile systems could also lead to war. All this requires the greatest vigilance by our armed forces, our government and political and military leadership so that war is not allowed to start by accident."

When Marshal Sokolovsky and his collaborators urge vigilance on their government and high command, they are dealing with one side of the problem: what the Soviet Union will do if such an event takes place. But the Soviet Government has a strong interest, to say the least, in preventing accident as well as in ensuring that its own response is consistent with its national interests. In Marshal Sokolovsky's example, there are clearly imperatives for the American as well as the Soviet Government—both in minimizing the chance of accident and in ensuring that the response is appropriate to the circumstances. The entire world has an evident interest in an organization of nuclear forces in which accidents will be unlikely, in which there will be an early and accurate recognition that what happened was an accident, and in which what happens next will be based on these facts.

Although these international interests are obvious, governments in present circumstances* are not going to talk to anyone about their system of control over nuclear weapons. The place where the power of decision on the firing of nuclear weapons has been settled from time to time will always be a closely guarded secret. Nevertheless, governments have a profound interest in being able to convince those who might retaliate that whatever has happened was not hostile in intent. The means of achieving this are fundamentally

* The circumstances in which this might be altered will be explored in Chapter 7.

technical and must obviously exploit the instantaneous character of modern communications to convey reassurance. But in such great matters reliable assurances are very difficult to achieve. The size of the problem should not be underrated. Designing against accidents is an insurance function: and all insurance companies insist that there are such things as uninsurable risks. Too much is at stake on the question of accidents to accept this as the solution.

The danger of a disastrous response to a nuclear accident is greatly diminished by a secure confrontation in which all sides know they cannot be disarmed. A power which has been the object of some curious and isolated attack is least likely to react if it knows that: (a) it cannot be disarmed; and (b) it cannot disarm its rival or rivals by a sudden and overwhelming attack and that, indeed, such a strike is unlikely to make a significant difference to the outcome of a major war. This is one of the many arguments for the strategically decisive if morally curious proposition that a central objective of international security is to make the world safe for strategic nuclear weapons.

There may also be important advantages to be gained from an active dialogue about nuclear forces in general and about the problem of accident in particular. The more military planners know about the forces and believe they know about the strategic thinking of their rivals the more readily they will doubt that some event can be the outbreak of calamitous hostilities. Study and thought about the problem of accident itself will make this a prominent possibility when those in authority are trying to understand what has happened. It will also help to persuade those who are designing nuclear systems that nothing is gained and everything can be lost by allowing the right to respond to pass to an uninformed military level.

These difficulties will become much more severe in the event of armed conflict of some kind. Here the danger of accident or of dangerous military initiative will increase greatly. Another problem will also emerge: this will be to give the assurance that certain things have not happened. When these problems are studied, it becomes obvious that major powers have a continuing need for good intelligence in the hands of their rivals, even in time of conflict and war. Indeed, this has become a permanently operating factor in international life. An international security institution that makes a real contribution to knowledge will have found permanent sources of strength and support: it will also be about the business of building world security.

IV *Chemical and biological weapons*

What are now regarded as unorthodox weapons—chemical, biological, environmental, and others—provide a field of urgent and important work for the servants of international security. The objective here is essentially one of keeping these weapons from the armouries and war plans of states. This is not going to be achieved by declarations or even treaties. It requires extensive regulations, carefully developed and enforced. Much scientific research has important military implications. The major powers are aware of this: but as with nuclear proliferation they feel a sense of futility in the face of a world order with so many states and so few means of bringing an order to bear.

The British Government has argued, with much justice, that biological weapons are a suitable subject for immediate international action. It has been seeking a treaty banning possession as a complement to the Geneva Protocol which bans their use. This class of weapons offers an almost ideal subject for international action: it is not widely stockpiled and those who have developed the weapons do not want to use them; the weapons themselves are open to the military objection that they take time to work; and (as with nuclear tests) the deep instinct of the species against plague and poison is working in favour of control. But it is clear that a general convention must be backed up by continuous definition and a serious administration. Otherwise, it could become a screen behind which one or more powers came to mobilize the full military potential of modern medical advances while more amiable peoples deceived themselves that they were safe.

The character of the threat and the most hopeful line of reform were put impressively and with authority by Dr. Joshua Lederberg of the United States, at an informal meeting of the C.C.D. in Geneva on 5 August 1970.* He stated his concern that predictable scientific advances would result in a transformation of the doctrine that biological weapons are unreliable. "The potential undoubtedly exists for the design and development of infective agents against which no credible defence is possible, through the genetic and chemical manipulation of these agents." After describing some of the possibilities that are developing, he went on to argue that great biological dangers to the human race still exist and that there are immense gaps in the international co-operative defences. The need to fight this menace and the need for verification of a biological warfare convention led, in his view, to a common institutional requirement:†

"The promulgation of an international agreement to control biological warfare in a negative sense should, therefore, be accompanied by steps urgently needed to build positive efforts at international co-operation, a kind of defensive biological research against natural enemies of the human species. One of the best assurances that any country might have that the microbiological research of its neighbours was directed towards human purposes would be constantly expanding participation in international health programmes. Any country that publicly and avowedly subscribed to the total renunciation of secret BW research might conceivably be able to continue clandestine efforts without revealing their substantial content. It would, however, have great difficulty in maintaining such an effort, at any substantial level or quality of operation, while still keeping its very existence secret. This applies especially to those among its own citizens who are specialists in health-oriented research and who are deeply involved in furthering health research activities within the framework of the international community. Therefore, besides the obvious direct health benefits

* His text was published by the Conference of the Committee on Disarmament as CCD/312, 27 August 1970.
† Ibid., pp. 7-8.

of expanded international co-operation we would also be rewarded by a higher level of mutual assurance that every party was indeed living up to the spirit of its obligations under a BW convention."

Chemical weapons pose different problems because they are already stockpiled in such quantities and because governments have begun to confuse the definitions. The American view differs from the publicly expressed opinions of most other governments; and it is obvious that nothing is going to happen on a world scale when so important a power as the United States is not prepared to go along with it. The Vietnam war has shown, however, that while the U.S. government is determined to use chemical weapons such as CS and CN gas, it is as unwilling to use mass killers like nerve gases as to use nuclear explosives. It is also, no doubt, profoundly afraid of encountering an enemy—particularly a guerrilla enemy—who is prepared to use these weapons on American troops.

Chemical weapons need the kind of common analysis which the scientists did for U Thant on a sustaining basis: and beyond this they need determined political-military planning in association with the professional planners of the decisive powers. As general principles are agreed and put into regulations, the techniques of verification may well have to extend very far and deep. While an issue like this may arouse small-power self-consciousness (especially if there is increasing talk about chemical and biological weapons as the poor man's nuclear weapons), it should not be difficult to show small powers that they share an international security interest in providing an effective system. Whether or not they are poor men's nuclear weapons, they could add greatly to the destructive character of poor men's as well as rich men's wars.

*   *   *

While this group of undertakings is undoubtedly ambitious and demanding, it does not go far beyond the problems which are already recognized to be the general concern of the world order. Each involves a developing agency or administration working to achieve agreements on issues of common interest and hoping gradually to influence the thinking and actions of governments. The obvious early tasks for international security institutions are to gain the best possible control of these exotic modern weapons. Because of their destructive power, and also because of their unknown future, these confer general insecurity. The fear of this insecurity should provide the political energy to bring a growing range of regulations into effect and through them to subject these new technologies to international control.

7

THE NOTION OF
COMMITMENT

AN international security structure which claims to be the
agent and trustee of world security as a whole cannot for long
confine itself to the essentially political, scientific and industrial problems of nuclear power or of chemical and biological
weapons. There remain the immense security problems
created by the world's armed forces and the great armouries
of weapons. However unsatisfactory the official plans for the
reform of power may be, they bring all armed forces within
their scope. A world security structure such as is contemplated
here must move step by step, allowing its authority to grow as
it gains the confidence of an effective consensus of states; but a
new approach to these problems cannot be seriously considered if it does not show how it would handle the traditional
problems of military power if a consensus emerged.

Two main issues arise. The first is to find a long-term
solution to the organization of nuclear weapons which can
preserve the security they are thought to provide. The second
is to construct a system of international security which can
be extended widely. Obviously, the achievement of either
objective will be the work of decades and the fruit of immense
political skill and effort. Earlier chapters have also subjected
it to certain limits: it cannot and will not come from the
establishment of some central monopoly of power; it will
always be subject to the ability of the greatest powers (at
least) to take their own security back into their own hands;
and it must be developed on the basis of the present system of
security. On these assumptions, how can governments
anxious to develop a working international system move
forward?

The answer is to find technical and military arrangements

in which states can subject part or all of their military forces to common organization while retaining ultimate ownership and control of these forces in their own hands. This would require the invention and refinement of a political and military device by which forces could have a dual character: national recruitment, pay and purposes combined with international planning and organization. The technique proposed here is that, where possible, armed forces should be committed or assigned to the international security structures. To the extent that national governments could see that their security objectives were being achieved by the collective body, they would commit their forces to it; to the extent that they felt they must use their forces for purposes inconsistent with the international arrangements, they would maintain them under purely national control. Although this suggestion may sound theoretical and unrealistic, the technique has been developed and refined in the orthodox military atmosphere of the North Atlantic Treaty Organization and has been practiced there for nearly 20 years.*

N.A.T.O. uses two words—commitment and assignment—to refer to those forces which are subject to common planning and considered to be available for the common tasks. The committed forces are under national peacetime command while the assigned forces are already within the international command structure; but in both cases the troops are supposed to be trained and equipped for the common requirement and are nevertheless subject to withdrawal at any time by national authorities. So long as governments share in the political and military purposes of the alliance, they see no contradiction in committing troops to this allied military structure. The forces remain fully national in organization, finance and command; and yet it is recognized that, at least for the

* The notion of commitment is also established as part of the security system foreseen by the authors of the United Nations Charter. Article 43 reads: "1. All Members of the United Nations, in order to contribute to the maintenance of international peace and security, undertake to make available to the Security Council, on its call and in accordance with a special agreement of agreements, armed forces, assistance, and facilities, including rights of passage, necessary for the purpose of maintaining international peace and security. . . . "

present, their most effective value to the nation is to be subject to international planning and organization.

In spite of the fact that the national authorities are fundamental in every legal and constitutional sense, a system of commitment can be an important political and military reality. Governments which are far from contemplating political union with one another have shown themselves ready to submit to it over many years. They know they are surrendering nothing they cannot reclaim and they have strong reasons for working together. They believe that the common commands (in which their officers participate) are engaged in assessing and identifying security interests best pursued in common. A number of weak states in Western Europe feel remarkably secure because of the existence of this structure. The commitment of forces as the reflection and agent of the commitment of governments has given the small the sense that they have the strength of the large, and the group as a whole the ability to define and protect its common interests.

Though not emphasized in public policy, the right of withdrawal has been carefully secured by N.A.T.O. governments. Their main anxiety was the risk of being committed to war by the common deployment and common commands. At the same time, the allied commanders have been fearful of a failure of nerve by one or more governments in the face of a serious conflict. These would not be problems in an international structure which included rivals or potential rivals. Nevertheless, the assurance of rights of withdrawal in both a legal and technical sense would probably be even more important than it has been in N.A.T.O. Great powers, and in many cases small powers, would know that the containment of their rivals still lay on them. On the reasonable assumption that the United States and Soviet Union (or N.A.T.O. and the Warsaw Pact) will still fear each other's power, their security will still depend on their ultimate capacity to deter and defend. The same will be true of many others. National security authorities must maintain their strength and their viability while they think they face threats of some kind. There is nevertheless no reason why they should not maintain much or all of the necessary strength in committed forces.

The premise of this argument is that there is a national security interest and a world security interest: both are proper objectives of national policy. A second premise is that the same troops can serve both objectives just as the same troops have served both national and alliance objectives in the N.A.T.O. countries. There is more than mere co-ordination in this. The opportunity to organize armed forces and influence their shape and character in rival countries through a common effort can offer world security the means to fulfil the objectives of national security.

*   *   *

Before passing to a general consideration of how the principles of commitment might be applied, it is reasonable to consider what long-term solution there might be to the problems posed by the existence of nuclear weapons. It has been argued in earlier chapters that nuclear weapons cannot and will not be abolished; and that a central nuclear monopoly is unrealistic and undesirable. Anyone putting forward such arguments has a basic obligation to show just what kind of nuclear organization is conceivable in favourable circumstances and to offer some image of an ideal world against which present proposals might be measured. At the same time, the proposals for nuclear weapons will be an important part of the definition of the system itself. Nothing in politics can be permanent; but it is reasonable to ask how in any reform of power the destructive possibilities of nuclear weapons and their steady proliferation are to be contained. One may also ask whether the apparent stability they now confer must be sacrificed.

The long-term objective proposed here is intended to organize these weapons while retaining their role of deterrence, such as it is. The suggestion is that the nuclear powers should commit (and eventually assign) their strategic nuclear forces to the international security organization. This should be done under procedures whereby ultimate control over the forces would be kept in national hands based on a stated legal right of withdrawal reinforced by the technical design and organization of the weapons themselves. A possible long-term arrangement may be illustrated by a simple contemporary example. Let us suppose a situation in which the Soviet Union and the United States each possessed 20 missile-firing submarines of the earlier Polaris type (16 single warhead missiles in the megaton range to each submarine); in which Britain, France and China each possessed five such submarines; and in which no other powers had decided to acquire nuclear weapons.* Let us suppose further that all 55 of these submarines were committed to the day-to-day management and planning of an international security authority. The terms of commitment would be that these forces could not be used by the international authorities without the approval of the governments owning and manning them; and that they could not be withdrawn by governments without a formal and public act. The primary duty of the international planners would be to see that no forces which could destroy these nuclear systems were created or maintained by anyone. Their invulnerability would be carefully preserved as a matter of deliberate and collective policy. Since governments would be able to order them back at any time under exclusively sovereign control, these five national states would know that they retained the physical capacity to wage nuclear war; they would know that neither they nor their rivals could use or threaten to use nuclear weapons without dissolving the international arrangements, simultaneously returning the forces of all the nuclear powers to sovereign national control; and they would have assurances amounting to certainty that no matter how heavily or deceptively they were attacked in war they could retaliate with certainty.†

In such a situation, a series of simultaneous benefits should be possible:

1. The powers concerned should know with certainty that

---

* A decision by other powers to develop nuclear weapons would not alter the principles of such a structure though every such decision would mean one more government and one more force to incorporate in it.

† One might ask if such a system might not fulfil a part of the prophecy of Raymond Aron: "Will historical man resemble the wolf that spares its kind, baring its throat as a sign of capitulation?", *Peace and War* (New York, Praeger).

they possessed an ultimate deterrent—an invulnerable force of thermonuclear weapons—and that in the act of joint planning they could make sure that their own forces could not be subject to surprise attack.

2. This deterrent would provide the physical certainty that the great powers and their allies could not be dominated by some real or notional central authority. This would found a plural world—with the advantages of variety, competition and sanctuary—on the facts of power. It would also give the decisive powers the sense of national security which they almost certainly need if they are to give their energies to the construction of world institutions.

3. If the system broke down, the present stability would remain, reinforced by the planned invulnerability of the heavy nuclear forces. This stability would prevail until such time as rearmament led to counterforce options in one or more of the powers—that is to say, until rearmament had proceeded to the point where a successful disarming attack seemed possible.

4. The day-to-day management of the nuclear forces by the international authorities could be designed to ensure that no accident could be confused with an operational use.

5. In a period of breakdown of civil order in a nuclear power, there would exist machinery for keeping the nuclear weapons out of the conflict by, in effect, leaving them with the international authorities to which they were normally assigned.

6. By concentrating attention on the active work of the international structure at so critical a point in the world order, the system could provide a unique source of prestige and authority for the international security institutions.

7. With time and success, the existence of the right of withdrawal might become remote, removing gradually the apparent difference between nuclear and non-nuclear powers and allowing common institutions to take what course might be thought appropriate to the conditions and consensus of the day.

A system organized along these lines contains an undeniable ambiguity, which exposes it to two different lines of criticism. The first comes from the orthodox, who argue that it is unthinkable for nations such as the United States or the Soviet Union to place their nuclear forces in the hands of an international body. The second comes as unfailingly from traditional reformers, who argue that forces remaining under ultimate national control are not international at all and that the proposed system is a fraud. There is something in each of these arguments. A structure of this kind would be designed to achieve two distinct and apparently contradictory objects: a stable confrontation of sovereign powers; and the gradual transfer of responsibility for keeping the peace to international institutions. But where nuclear weapons are concerned apparent contradictions are nothing new. They have created a situation in which world peace has been kept (or thought by many of those concerned to have been kept) through the fear that weapons that are essentially unusable will be used. They have forced national governments to pretend that they are irrational. They claim to have found security in a form of maximum insecurity. The orthodox-minded, in particular, are poorly placed to talk about contradictions when they themselves rely on theories of deterrence. In politics, the question is not whether we are faced with contradictions but whether, as a matter of practical administration, two objectives can be combined.

As the political benefits outlined above are being sought in what are essentially technical arrangements, it is perhaps desirable to attempt some definition of the technical objectives. The first of these is, of course, safety for the nuclear weapons themselves from every conceivable form of attack or sabotage. This question has already been extensively explored by governments and is discussed in Chapters 2 and 6. The hypothesis is that all powers have agreed to dismantle whatever forces are designed or might be used to attack the nuclear forces of others. If these purposes had been pursued with unity and consistency (and under the eyes of those being targeted) for some time it is impossible to see how they could fail to achieve their objectives. The notion of submarine forces as an appropriate long-term solution has been put forward here for illustrative purposes and because it is now the view of most powers that these provide a uniquely invulnerable group of mobile nuclear missile bases. It might equally be decided to maintain a land-based force, possible with active ballistic missile defences; or to develop another system; or (as is perhaps most likely) to maintain some mixture of these possibilities. However it was done, there would be no obvious problem in designing forces which could remain deterrents in being no matter what any other power (including the central authorities) might choose to do.

If the forces are maintained in a state of total mutual invulnerability, the efficiency of the arrangements for their return to total national control is not critical: *ex hypothesi* they cannot be destroyed. Nevertheless, the ideal would be a system in which the political realities were accurately mirrored in the technical facts. To achieve this, the system should have three main characteristics:

1. A physical inability to fire the assigned nuclear weapons without the expiry of an established period of notice.

2. The assurance of unimpeded national control for all powers after the expiry of this period.

3. Full and unfailing communication of the fact that a decision to reassert independence has been initiated.

There is a basic difficulty in inhibiting the freedom of action of governments in relation to their own nuclear weapons. The electronic control links and other methods now used to prevent the unauthorized use of nuclear weapons are designed to place the capacity to fire these weapons beyond the power of those in physical control of them. These men are professional service officers who must live a normal service life. They have few resources at their disposal. On the other hand, a structure that would offer certainty that all the resources available to a major government and its armed forces would not make it possible to fire well-designed nuclear weapons within a significant period—say, four days—would be a much more ambitious enterprise. One is dealing here with a wealthy government with the full resources of modern industry at its command. It cannot be assumed, therefore, that the problem would be easy to solve.

To achieve certain use after a period of time and total

inability to use before then, three obvious techniques suggest themselves: a coded signal which must be put into the weapons; a missing part; or an inevitably time-consuming process which must be gone through to make the weapons operational. No doubt there are other possibilities. Both the coded signal and the missing part suffer from the fact that the producers of the weapons would have ample opportunity to know all their characteristics. To be reliable, the coding would have to be established by an authority outside the country which owned the weapons—presumably by an establishment operated internationally. It would also have to be clear that no one had designed a method of circumventing the coding in his own weapons. Solutions of this kind are unlikely to be trusted by national defence establishments.

The most promising method is probably the time-consuming process. Skilled designers might be able to solve the problem of adjusting submarine-based weapons (for example) in such a way as to impose a minimum period of work before they could be fired. It is conceivable that after a long period the withdrawal time might be increased by the maintenance of prime weapons in what might amount to an unassembled condition. This would depend, of course, on their continuing total invulnerability. Such arrangements could perhaps be presented as a form of nuclear disarmament: but it would be one in which sophisticated modern nuclear weapons systems safe from each other's power would still lie behind the international order and in which their possessors' sovereignty could not be challenged without the risk of suicidal war.

The forces would be maintained by officers and crews of the states owning them. Nevertheless, the needs of a world structure would probably dictate a system under which the world organization would have its own men with their own communications associated with the weapons. This should be a simple matter with land-based weapons. The inhibitions on transmissions of any kind from ballistic missile submarines create real problems, but these could be relaxed once the forces capable of destroying the submarines had been dismantled. A check of this kind would make it possible to give continuous guarantees to all governments about the state of the world's nuclear forces; and in time this should remove all urgency from individual dispositions. It would also provide a complete and reliable solution to the problem of accidental firing or of the unidentified use of a nuclear weapon. There are many reasons why governments should welcome such arrangements in relation to their own weapons (not least that they would extend to rivals' weapons); but perhaps the most important is that they would then be in a position to give reliable assurances that some inexplicable event on a rival's territory was not an initiation of hostilities by them. No national interest is greater than to be able to show that (contrary to what potential enemies may for some reason think) you have not fired nuclear weapons, or have not done so deliberately.

Strategic arms limitation of the kind discussed in Chapter 6 would indicate the appropriate first moves towards a structure of this kind. Commitment and assignment would enable this process to go forward to whatever point the governments concerned chose. The original act of commitment would imply that the function and use of these particular forces had become ₍a proper subject for collective expert study and recommendation. Nothing much would be seen to happen. The nuclear powers would be stating their readiness to develop a joint operational planning and control system provided this was seen at every stage to be consistent with national security. The duty of the common organization would then be to persuade governments to accept the directives on which a conscious and secure organization of strategic nuclear forces could take place.

At an appropriate stage in this process, the N.A.T.O. distinction of commitment and assignment might usefully be introduced. The core of heavy nuclear forces would be the leading candidates for assignment since they would be permanently maintained as the protected favourite of the system. Once an acceptable joint command was established, they might be put gradually under its day-to-day operational control and organization. The duties of the command would be exceptionally clear: to maintain all the forces assigned in a state of total invulnerability. To a considerable extent, of course, this would depend not on what happened to the forces themselves but on the dispositions of the forces which might threaten them, whether nuclear or conventional. The development of a secure assigned force would require constant negotiation by the central authorities in which they might hope to stimulate bargains among the affected powers.

There are, of course, many kinds of nuclear forces. Governments would be obliged to ask themselves what they were getting from their nuclear weapons and what they might hope to get in the future. The reform of power towards a simple nuclear system of the kind suggested here could only be achieved through the gradual abandonment of a number of important functions now performed by nuclear forces. Forces which exist to increase the dangers of local conventional war (as some argue N.A.T.O. tactical nuclear weapons now do) would be inconsistent with such a system, as would forces designed to limit damage by taking out rival nuclear forces on the ground or by intercepting them in the air. These might be committed to a common structure as part of the larger military confrontation in which they play a part; and over a period of time it might be possible to reduce them mutually.

A system of this kind would have great advantages to the nuclear powers. It should increase their security by guaranteeing the effectiveness of their strategic nuclear forces; and it should save them a great deal of money and effort. For these reasons, and because the objectives themselves are straightforward the perfection of the strategic arms confrontation should prove to be one of the simpler duties of a world security agency, provided all the nuclear powers are reconciled to it.*

*　　*　　*

* One can foresee severe difficulties in getting the more advanced nuclear powers to forgo any defensive or disarming capability they might feel they possessed and also in persuading other nuclear powers to agree to some long-term numerical inferiority. This second requirement is not essential—indeed, governments would in principle be free to expand their forces—but it might be a necessary condition in practice to persuade the United States and the Soviet Union to join in the development of such a system.

A more subtle and more political problem is to organize nuclear weapons in such a way as to minimize the incentive of non-nuclear states to acquire them. Under the suggested system, as at present, decisions to build national nuclear forces will be determined by the balance of the advantages (mainly in ultimate security) against the disadvantages (mainly cost). International arrangements are likely to discourage nuclear proliferation to the extent that they increase security. Proliferation could also be discouraged if new arrangements made materials and delivery systems more difficult or more expensive. To the extent, however, that they guarantee the effectiveness of strategic nuclear forces—and this is an essential objective—they will undoubtedly make the problem of national nuclear weapons less difficult for middle and even small powers. This is an undoubted disadvantage in a reform of power along the lines suggested here. It may, however, be an advantage to the non-nuclear powers which in practice they would not be likely to exploit. If a growing number of powers chose to develop nuclear weapons in the favourable circumstances created by planners working on the principles outlined above, it is likely that the major powers would be forced to react. They could be expected to acquire a capacity to strike at those forces or defend their own territory against them. No doubt the resulting system could be given a secure international structure once its objectives had been generally defined and acknowledged; but a relatively simple system of the kind suggested probably depends on restraint by the non-nuclear powers.

The key to their restraint in such a system (as outside it) is their perception of the security order in which they find themselves. If they think they are reasonably safe without nuclear weapons, and will be indefinitely, they are unlikely to want to spend the resources. Can international institutions produce this sense? This is a basic question: and it is one which must be looked at very carefully because the traditional answer—that the necessary guarantees must come either from the institution itself or from individual countries—can obscure the truth.

The idea that a central institution should itself be the

source of security goes along with notions, conscious or unconscious, of world government. Many millions of people expected the League of Nations to handle aggressors and have hoped for the same thing from the U.N. Where nuclear weapons are concerned, this line of argument leads to suggestions that a nuclear force should ultimately be placed in the hands of a central authority with the undertaking that it would be used without fail in retaliation on behalf of any member state which was attacked. Similar notions have been put forward in the N.A.T.O. grouping. It can be said in support of this "world deterrent" or "U.N. deterrent" school that the use of nuclear weapons by the central institutions would not threaten the nuclear powers with a potentially suicidal war against their will—as it would with N.A.T.O. The world body as such would have no population; and if it had its nuclear forces in a form (such as submarines) in which they could not be struck it would presumably be free from the threat of retaliation. Provided the institutions had the will and capacity for decision, this would thus constitute a threat of a special and particularly awesome character. But these possibilities merely increase the certainty that no such centre of authority will be created.

The second and more realistic notion is that guarantees must come from the nuclear powers themselves and must therefore be purely national, as they are believed to be now. It is clear that even in a committed and assigned system of nuclear weapons, the only authority which will have the power to give the order to fire is the government owning the weapons. Thus if the weapons of the nuclear powers are to play some part in the security of the non-nuclear powers, it appears to follow that the guarantees must be made by individual countries. This was the assumption made by the United States, the Soviet Union and the United Kingdom in trying to put some form of guarantee structure behind the Non-Proliferation Treaty. The three of them read statements to the Security Council on 17 June 1968,* whose wording was summed up in a Security Council resolution two days later:

"The Security Council. . . .

* See U.N. Document S/PV. 1430.

"2. Welcomes the intention expressed by certain States that they will provide or support immediate assistance, in accordance with the Charter, to any non-nuclear weapon State Party to the Treaty on the Non-Proliferation of Nuclear Weapons that is a victim of an act or an object of a threat of aggression in which nuclear weapons are used."

The weakness and qualifications in this wording are evidence enough, however, of how little security is likely to be transmitted from the powerful to the weak through general proclamations. The Security Council exercise was a valiant effort at international security—at, in effect, some semblance of a contract to justify the discrimination in the Non-Proliferation Treaty—and it has certainly done no harm. It could acquire real meaning if it was used as the basis for a dramatic great power response to some nuclear threat. As it stands, however, the declaration is unlikely to change the varying views of non-nuclear powers about how much they can count on others in a national emergency. The same limitations are likely to apply to any general verbal commitments. The persistent doubts in the mind of the government of Israel about the various undertakings which have been given from time to time by the United States are those which any realistic government will feel. Equally, the United States is bound to stop far short of irreversible commitments to a country which could involve it in an exceptionally serious situation without having taken into account the larger issues facing the United States.

The best example of an American guarantee is the one which is extended to the Federal Republic of Germany. Here it is recognized that the guarantor is involved in the whole security life of the area he is guaranteeing. Bonn governments do not expect to be able to launch their army without American approval, as the Israelis do. The two work together at the details of their security policy through close political co-operation and the N.A.T.O. military structure.

This suggests the true answer to the problem of guarantees. The question about whether they should come from the collective institution or from individual countries is misleading. Neither alone can offer anything that will look like a guarantee to a non-nuclear country. Only the individual country using an international institution to create a close and genuine security relationship can really convey the power of the big into the defence of the poor. The two must march together.

The evidence is, therefore, that in a dangerous age the power of the strong is only likely to be available to the weak if they have a close institutional relationship. The power must come bilaterally because no major power is going to place its armed forces at the free disposal of others. But that power must be shared in a relationship in which the weak identify with the strong and both can align their policies towards common objects. This is what Germans and Americans do in N.A.T.O. If the great powers are to build a world in which small states will feel secure, they will need a real sense of community combined with institutions to give it life. That will most easily come about—indeed, it may only come about— through identification with a common security order. This has, of course, happened in N.A.T.O. and elsewhere, though always on an apparently temporary basis. But countries like Japan, India, Israel, Mexico, Brazil, Sweden and many others who consider themselves non-aligned are outside even these arrangements and seem likely to remain so. A world institution could create a vehicle of political commitment for such countries. If, on the other hand, the great powers were to construct a common system in order to give themselves a safer and cheaper life and took the occasion to cut what they regard as the burden of their commitments, they could well improve their own military relations while inadvertently stimulating the proliferation which would wreck their system. A world order will be built and sustained primarily by the great powers. But because it is a world order, and because it is many small states' best hope of security, it can attach the small and medium to the large. This alone will make the discrimination of the N.P.T. a legitimate and enduring contract.

*   *   *

The strategic nuclear weapons problem, however awesome,

remains simple in its fundamentals. Its political content is remarkably small once states are genuinely ready to renounce a disarming capability against others. From a few decisions of principle, good international military planners should be able to reach an acceptable range of conclusions. Partly this is because these weapons are so destructive as to be outside the political calculations which are the basis for most international disputes. Partly it is because, in the words of Mr. Robert McNamara, "in contrast to most other military requirements, the requirement for strategic retaliatory forces lends itself rather well to reasonably precise calculation". It is as we recede from nuclear weapons to the weapons which are the servants of political policy that the most demanding problems of world security undoubtedly emerge.

Here the basic principles already outlined would seem to apply unchanged. First, the object is to gain a commitment to common organization of the forces that are capable of waging war and to try to influence their development in accordance with appropriate doctrines of world security. Second, the right of withdrawal is fundamental. Third, the duty of confronting and (if necessary) waging war against major forces which have been withdrawn falls on states and not on the world organization itself.

Commitment in these circumstances becomes an act of willingness to seek international solutions rather than a solution in itself. In this sense, one might say that the members of the General Agreement on Tariffs and Trade have committed their tariffs to the G.A.T.T.: they have, in effect, subjected them to the criticisms and policy proposals of a common body with a general intention of achieving more liberal trade policies. They do not guarantee any particular result when they make this commitment: they retain the right to return to strong protectionism should they think this necessary; but they recognize that they share a common interest with other states in freer world trade. The commitment of armed forces would in this sense constitute a statement of intent about using those forces in support of world security if this could be shown to be consistent with the government's definition of the national security interest. Only time and detailed proposals can demonstrate this.

The act of commitment of units might be associated with an elemental series of obligations designed to give the international organization a basis for planning. While it has been argued* that membership in any organization trying to organize world security should involve an undertaking to give evidence in good faith about national defence policy, this would apply with particular force to committed units. Their role and armaments would be declared in detail; and they would become a legitimate subject for recommendation by the professional organization or for criticism by rivals. In effect, a dialogue would begin between the national authorities responsible for these units and the international authorities whose duty it would be to work for the removal of any insecurity they may be causing to others. The object would be to provoke alterations in policy which would increase general security.

The early acts of commitment could be combined with efforts to create a world security consciousness. Troops might wear a particular flash; various publicity techniques could be used to create a common consciousness; a discreet range of cross-posting and joint exercising could be developed which would increase the appeal of service life in particular countries. More substantially, the international organization might gradually take over from the old imperial centres the task of training officers and running staff courses and technical schools. These would obviously be of most interest to the small and poor countries, where a strong sense of identity with world security institutions will most easily emerge. If colleges of this kind could be brought up to a high level, they would produce their own kind of man who could work easily on international staffs or on peace-keeping. These advantages are already to be found in the British links with many Commonwealth armed forces, which have provided the small and poor with the officers and specialists they needed and have also been the basis for effective co-operation in war and in U.N. peace-keeping. Of course, the Commonwealth

* See Chapter 5.

has many advantages. A common language is very useful; and the fact that Commonwealth armed forces are the direct heirs of colonial forces (and the Indian Army) puts all the strength of military conservatism behind the system. Nevertheless, it is a model; it shows what the small and poor require; and the Commonwealth arrangements are themselves available to form part of something with world patronage and support. Such an activity could give enduring strength to a world system.

Orthodox western disarmament thought has always looked to the international recruitment and command of armed forces. It conceives an ideal solution in which the maintenance of peace will be the responsibility of an international executive, commanding commonly financed and recruited forces in the service of laws made by common institutions. While this may conceivably prove to be appropriate to some changed world in future, there is little to be gained by trying to build an international security system on these foundations. The world order is now being sustained by vast and expensive military forces commanded and financed by national governments and served by the scientific and industrial strength of great nations; if there is a threat to world security, these pose it; if there is an answer to this threat, these provide it. There may or may not be a case for a United Nations force of 50,000 or 100,000 men for particular purposes: though there is no sign that the conditions exist in which the raising, financing or command of such a force would be practical politics. Mr. Brian Urquhart, a senior U.N. official who did as much as anyone to make U.N. peace-keeping a reality, put his personal authority against such a step in 1964.* "The institutional addition at this time of a permanent international police force would in all probability worsen the state of international politics, and it might, by its very existence or through precipitate and inappropriate use, complicate the very situations it was designed to solve." At some later date, such troops might be useful in the performance of limited services; but the basic security problems are posed by the vast

* *International Military Forces*, ed. Lincoln Bloomfield (Boston, Little, Brown, 1964), p. 141.

array of men and weapons possessed by national governments and by the potential for military force which is a permanent part of all populations and civil industries. These cannot be dominated by any foreseeable international force and they alone can form the basis of an international security system.

On the other hand, the notion of assignment, which has already played an important part in the life of the United Nations, could be expanded beyond the specific requirements of peace-keeping. An international security institution which saw its primary work in ordering the security systems of its members could well find it useful to accept the assignment of armed forces for purposes far beyond peace-keeping. If a broad and far-reaching development of the authority of the centre became acceptable and desirable, the technique of assignment could become the vehicle for gradually shifting the centre of responsibility for world security. At this stage, such speculation can go no further. This is not a suitable subject for grand designs. An international system will extend its authority and responsibility in relation to need and as the effective consensus permits. To try to project how this might happen is to become theoretical and almost certainly irrelevant.

A fundamental question—many would say the fundamental question—is the extent of the responsibility of the international authorities for maintaining world security in the face of armed challenges. It has already been argued that there can be no question of world responsibility for the discipline of a great power. This premise is, in effect, accepted in the Charter of the United Nations which nevertheless contemplates U.N. Security Council action against lesser states where the five permanent members are unanimous. The U.N. began as a military alliance; and the notion of collective security in the sense of unity against the transgressor still underlies it. U.N. practice, however, has been very different. Its peace-keeping operations have required the agreement of the government on whose territory they are to be conducted and have limited military action, in general, to the defence of U.N. troops themselves and their communications.*

* See Brian Urquhart, ibid., for an outstanding account of the problem of U.N. peace-keeping and valuable essays by others covering most of

These two U.N. positions form, in effect, the outer limits of realistic international action. Either such action can take place where no major power is prepared to oppose it; or it can be confined to what all the relevant governments will support. The experience of the United Nations suggests that anything but the second is still beyond the capacity of international society. To take an obvious case, all the major powers and almost all other states are agreed that Britain is the sovereign power in Rhodesia, that the 1965 declaration of independence by the Smith government was illegal, and that the continuation of this illegal situation is bad for Rhodesia and for the world. The power of the Smith government rests on less than 300,000 whites. If it is supported militarily by the South African white population, the two together total less than four million. Yet the U.N. has been unwilling to contemplate an enforcement action even of this magnitude.

The notion of enforcement has played a pernicious part in speculation about disarmament and international organization because of an essentially deceptive lawyer's approach to authority in national states. While states do from time to time (in Burke's phrase) draw up an indictment against a whole people—the United States did against the Confederacy, Nigeria did against Biafra—they usually understand that the fight for the union is really a civil war between two parts of the state. The normal practice in national states is to incorporate large units in the consensus by the familiar techniques of politics. An international system in which states are seen as subjects whose obedience to the central law-making authorities is fundamental will not be established and could not endure. One in which they are seen as legislators, participating in the consensus and accepting reasonable compromises in the general interest, is the only realistic hope. It suggests very different criteria.

Some enforcement may, of course, be necessary. The

---

the problems raised by these experiments. In the Congo operation, mounted in 1960, Security Council directives allowed the use of force for self-defence, to prevent civil war, and in the last resort to apprehend foreign military personnel.

development of a form of international piracy in the air could produce a sufficient international determination to stamp it out. A breach of an international system to control biological weapons might well inflame international society as a whole to the point where it would take collective action to protect itself. Technology is steadily adding to the mischief which a determined wrecker could practice and from time to time this may have to be faced. The growth of a wide area of agreed military practice could well provide the basis for a parallel growth of the notion of the outlaw state. If an effective consensus of the Powers wanted to move in this way, there would be no shortage of legal power in Chapter 7 of the U.N. Charter. The American attitude to Cuba in the early days of the Castro revolution or the Soviet Union's attitude to Czechoslovakia under the Dubcek régime show that the two greatest powers are easily persuaded that certain forms of state in certain places are intolerable. With some modifications in the international order, it is conceivable that certain types of state might attract the fear and hostility of many powers. This is a matter for the effective consensus and not for the constitution of the international system itself. A good working premise is that enforcement will seldom be the duty or task of an international security system and that to make it the prime criterion of success—as the League of Nations did and as many have of the Security Council—is to miss the main point and ask the impossible.

The central work of a world security authority must come where the world interest is most easily aligned with national interests. There is a collective interest in almost every situation, both in peace and in war, which even those confronting each other recognize from time to time. In a peaceful confrontation in which both sides are deployed defensively (such as that which prevails in Central Europe), the situation provides possibilities for joint planners seeking to achieve the objectives of both sides. Much useful speculation along these lines has taken place in the hope that it might lead to treaties or informal agreements thinning out forces or modifying armaments. Unfortunately, these mechanisms are unsuited to the problem. A real reform of European security undoubtedly requires a common institution of high military quality, issuing and enforcing agreed directives and developing a conscious system of security from the requirements of the two alliances.

The process of commitment of forces to international security authorities would undoubtedly be lengthy. What might be foreseen eventually, however, is the commitment of both sides in a conflicting situation—in effect, a commitment of the situation itself—at the choice of those concerned. Such an arrangement has already been defended as the best solution to the thermonuclear weapons problem. Military structures linked to a political conflict can be expected to lose their importance if for some reason political solutions are found. They must be maintained safely until then, accepting (as the U.N. has been forced to accept) that the peacekeeper can prolong the conflict by making a resolution less necessary. Of course, if one side has hopes of a military solution, as in the Nigerian conflict with Biafra, it will not choose to commit its forces. But in most of the disputes which have built up heavy armaments on both sides (Berlin and Germany, the Israeli frontiers, Kashmir, strategic nuclear arms) neither side has had great hopes of achieving a solution by force. Both must, however, be certain that they can handle the situation should the other side resort to force. In principle, a situation in which both sides are essentially defensive in their dispositions offers international security promising material on which to work.

We must also anticipate that new disputes will develop from time to time. A security order of this kind cannot hope to solve the current batch of problems and then relax. Armed forces will grow around the infection of political conflict wherever it may arise. Who forecast in the 1950s that by the mid-1960s China and India would be disputing the ownership of a vast unoccupied area of Asia or that Indonesia would be threatening force against Malaysia? Each of these disputes generated increased armed forces. Their resolution reduced the forces again. A world security institution would have to live with ceaseless repetitions of this type of situation, no doubt taking many forms.

It may well be asked whether such an institution in such circumstances could perform any useful function. The answer must turn primarily on the attitude of the major powers and of those other powers which share their world view. In one form or another, their presence is a fact in most situations: and the nature of their involvement now determines, and probably always will determine, the part played by international society as a whole. In this respect, we may divide local conflict situations into four broad classes:

1. A fight for superiority by two or more lesser powers in which the major powers are unwilling to intervene. A typical example of this is the India-Pakistan conflict over Kashmir. It is unlikely that an international security organization would be ready to intervene in such a situation, though once the parties both wanted an armistice or settlement it could have an important role.

2. A local conflict in which one major power is a participant. Examples of this are the Vietnam situation in the middle and late 1960s and the Soviet–Hungarian and Warsaw Pact–Czech confrontations of 1956 and 1968. Clearly, an international security organization would be unable to intervene in such situations.

3. A local conflict in which two major powers are prepared to intervene on opposite sides. It was believed by many that this might be the situation in the Congo in 1960 and also during the Cyprus crisis of 1964.

4. A local conflict in which the major powers can perceive a common interest. This can derive (perhaps paradoxically) from an anxiety to avoid the dangers of involvement on different sides and the resulting need to provide guarantees that the situation will not disintegrate to the point where one might be forced to intervene. It can also accompany a weakening of the resolve to fight among smaller states, either because of the costs involved or because the objectives have been achieved (or seem impossible to achieve). This is the most hopeful sphere of action for an organization recognizing that it is not an agency of enforcement except in special circumstances.

One noticeable characteristic of conflict in our time is the growth of the conscious and even institutional interplay of the national and the collective interest. The confrontation between the United States and North Vietnam has been conducted in its later stages with a peace conference running simultaneously with the war. This had earlier happened in Korea. In both cases, the search for a joint solution began when the hopes of total victory began to fade on both sides. The Cuban missile crisis was a virtually instant combination of military moves towards confrontation and diplomatic manoeuvring for minimum agreement. In situations like the India–Pakistan conflict or the Arab–Israel wars, the collective interest has taken the form of continuous attempts at influence by the external powers, and especially the major powers. Clearly in these situations a world security institution has the duty of serving the consensus and not of joining in the conflict. Where there is no consensus and no desire for one (as, for example, in the Soviet conflicts with Hungary or Czechoslovakia, the Nigerian conflict with Biafra, or the first five days of the Six Day War) it has no obvious function. Its duty is to wait for the desire for a minimum common policy and to serve this.

The possible alternation of confrontation and international action is perhaps best illustrated by the progress of Arab–Israeli relations through the various military trials both sides have undertaken. If the British can be seen (as they were by Zionists and Arabs) as a kind of international authority, the period of the Mandate was one of physical control from the outside. With the British withdrawal, the 1948 war broke out. As it progressed, both sides decided that they would like to settle on armistice lines. This brought United Nations planning into action. For various reasons, a new trial of force was undertaken in the 1956 Sinai campaign; but this soon led to a reassertion of international arrangements, with the U.N. peace-keeping forces and the Western guarantees (later forgotten) to Israel. Confrontation seemed the preferable course in 1967 to at least one and probably both of the rivals; but once more after a short trial of arms there was a need for a minimum common policy to control the situation. There is evidence that in most contemporary conflicts above the level of guerrilla war the risks are so great and the consumption of armaments so rapid that a shared interest in some form of settlement emerges at an early stage. The world is full of peacemakers ready and willing to make their good offices available; and their achievements in recent years have been remarkable. Nevertheless, it is likely that more could be done to find and exploit common interests by professional machinery with military expertise and a good reputation.

The Arab–Israeli cycle of confrontation and consensus is not one which anyone would like to see copied. But it illustrates the interplay of these two in relation to what is perhaps the most persistent contemporary conflict. It also shows the active and continuing part which those who confine themselves to consensus (like the U.N.) can take. We may return to the analogy with trade policy. An organization like the G.A.T.T. exists for the liberalization of world trade. Its objects are generally accepted by member states; but from time to time they find that their own particular interests must override the general, or they feel that the organization has seriously misunderstood just what the general interest is. They take national action; others may or may not retaliate; to some extent the operation of the institution is temporarily weakened. But if it has calculated its position correctly, and if the destruction of the machinery is avoided, the general interest comes in time to absorb the particular and governments find good reasons for falling back into line. This should be the mood of an international security institution, even when faced with open warfare.

An international security order can only be the sum of a great number of individual security situations. It may be that at times the states of the world, weary with detailed negotiation, will see some virtue in a general reduction of armed forces or in careful elimination of certain classes of weapons. But in general it is likely that a conscious international order will advance by detailed efforts to meet the anxieties of governments about security. The commitment of the sources of others' insecurity could give men devoted to this task a chance to show that a conscious world order is possible and can make the general desire for security into an enduring system.

In this way, world security could grow a new skin, and over the years the old one might die. As with any political artifice, success would depend on the skill and understanding of those who developed and worked it. There can be few clear outlines or anything like a blueprint. But there are basic requirements, most of which can be filled without asking governments to scrap their forces and weapons. A method of growth from the present must be found. And those who will examine the present carefully will find that the new growth is well under way—in the nascent atomic energy system, in defensive strategies, in second strike weapons systems, in the commitment of peace-keeping forces, in the careful calculations which the powers make in bargaining situations, in the attempt to stop the spread of nuclear weapons through some system of guarantees. A chess board is either black with white squares or white with black squares. In going from one to another, the board need not be changed at all. The powers similarly are now organized on a sovereign basis with international arrangements. They could go over to an international system with sovereign arrangements with no essential alteration in their present capacity to defend themselves and their allies. But they could create the technical and military context and perhaps the political conditions in which their common servants could achieve the common object of severely limiting or even abolishing war which may otherwise elude them.

THE POLITICAL CONTEXT

ONE of the distinguishing features of the twentieth century has been its concern with the reform of power. The Hague Conferences, which began on its eve, had an enduring effect on the laws of war and peace. The League of Nations and the United Nations were attempts to remedy the proven defects of the Concert of Europe. Virtually all governments have come to regard the operation of international security agencies as natural and normal, even though they are by no means clear about the rules which should be imposed or the forces that should be employed.

These attitudes have grown through a period of political-military disaster. Europe allowed herself to be ruled from 1914 to 1918 by power operating largely outside any real political context. Victory was a substitute for policy, and military technology made victory difficult to achieve. In the peace that followed the situation was reversed. The League of Nations was obliged to operate a political policy without the power on which to base it: and it fell easy prey to those who had equipped themselves with usable military force. The major powers stumbled forward in incomprehension: the British and French that it could all happen twice; the Germans and Japanese that they could be subjected to unbelievable destruction and retribution; the Americans that they should be preoccupied with building up the power of those who were thought to have been the cause of the disaster; the Soviet Union that she should be so feared and threatened over so long a period. Through all these experiences a new series of historical images and attitudes has emerged. Munich has become the symbol of a significant and influential view of history. So may the American view of the Cuban missile crisis of 1962. Each is now more familiar and more influential than the Concert of Europe. The impotence of the United Nations following the failure of the League has generated widespread hesitations about international organizations operating in the security field. The apparent safety of the main powers from attack in the quarter century of the atomic age has moderated their fears and discredited the prophets of doom or misfortune who must inevitably be the main proponents of reform.

In this context, the passion for the reform of power seems to be passing. Where the maintenance of the international system had for centuries been one of the primary concerns of governments, it is now the object of little serious speculation, either academic or governmental. Wild plans are put forward for public consumption while the needs of the system itself get little attention. By a tragic perversion of attitudes, those who speculate on disarmament (or even its milder variant of the late 1950s, arms control) are thought to be lacking in sophistication or realism.

This situation was tolerable while there was some form of working trusteeship for international society. In the period from 1945 until the 1960s, the grouping led by the Americans, British and French was able to find minimum solutions for most of the world's most pressing security problems. It was powerfully placed with the occupation régimes in Germany and Japan (later converted into N.A.T.O. and other effective security relationships), the British in much of Africa, the Persian Gulf and Malaysia, the Americans with some kind of working hemispheric system, and so on. They and their allies largely financed and worked the United Nations in uneasy co-operation with the Soviet Union; and they built up a powerful structure of influence based on prestige, money, trade and occasionally military power. Where initiatives were taken—in U.N.E.F., in the Congo or Cyprus, in the development of a safeguards system for nuclear materials, in rearming West Germany, in the Non-Proliferation Treaty—it was usually at the initiative of this group.

Gradually but unmistakably, however, the grouping has had a sense of loss of power. First France and then the United States and Britain have been disillusioned by their experiences outside the Atlantic area. While the group has grown stronger through the accession of Japan and most of Germany, the leadership of the President of the United States is less generally recognized. The Americans themselves have wearied of the complications of alliance relations and have preferred in Cuba and in Vietnam to operate without the familiar attempts to achieve a common policy. The Allies have also preferred it, welcoming the fact that the loss of power also meant a loss of responsibility.

It would be an exaggeration to say that this American-led system no longer exists. Where important security interests are at stake—particularly in Europe but also, if challenged, in Japan—it would undoubtedly respond with unity and determination. But for many purposes it cannot act because it is not comprehensive or unified enough. To manage an anti-proliferation system needs the co-operation of the Soviet bloc; to control the arms trade needs strong internal cohesion and discipline; to operate an effective Middle Eastern peace-keeping role probably needs both.

The great object of a reform of power must be to build a permanent structure able to bear the weight of maintaining the world order. In many of its essentials, this must be a great power system, since the largest powers now carry most of the weight and because their wealth and strength is so massive. But their power itself is dependent on operating through a broad consensus. The American sense of loss of power is not related to any significant relative loss of military strength or wealth. It went, however, with a tendency for the American alliance system to weaken and so with a decline in the effective points where American power could be made into policy. Many political systems have been based on domination: but there is normally a distinct element of reciprocity in which the more and the less powerful develop habits of co-operation that reflect the facts of power. The familiar Gaullist accusation that the western alliances have been agencies of American (or Anglo-Saxon) power and influence is undoubtedly well founded: but most of those who have taken part in these experiments have considered that they also served their own interests. A false antithesis is easily created. In international society as now constituted, the power of the few depends on the relations of the few with the many.

Experience suggests that the task of building a working order is primarily one of gaining the effective co-operation of the major powers. The United States, the Soviet Union, Britain, West Germany, India and Japan are obvious major participants. Lesser powers will follow where the major powers with which they have links give the lead. The first moves towards an international system for nuclear weapons have been based on the Soviet Union, the United States, Britain and their allies. These three negotiated the partial test ban and then invited general support (which was in large measure forthcoming). The N.P.T. was originally negotiated on a Soviet-American basis; and this formula was also used for the outer space treaty, the sea-bed treaty, and the negotiations on strategic arms limitations. In any search for an effective consensus, this grouping is obviously fundamental, as it is to the United Nations.

Although there was considerable and understandable resistance to the discrimination of the N.P.T. in a number of countries—notably India, Japan, Australia, West Germany and Brazil—the only two significant countries which have systematically resisted the development of this international security grouping are France and China. It may be doubted whether the French attitude is of consequence. France is essentially a *status quo* power and has been resisting the workings of what Soviet–American–British grouping there has been on the grounds that it implied American, or Anglo-American, representation of the countries of western Europe. Other Western Europe countries have not so far been prepared to accept this thesis. Nevertheless, there is a permanent danger that a Soviet–American attempt to construct an international security order will be seen by the main countries of Western Europe as an attempt to exclude them from control over their own destinies. In that event, France's essentially procedural argument will become more basic; and unless ways are found to reintroduce non-Communist Europe into the structure a really significant consensus will be impossible. The growing conviction in Washington and

Moscow that they can solve the problems together could well produce this result. The continuation of the technique used for the N.P.T. (which, as it happened, affected secondary powers much more than those who negotiated it) would leave the Soviet–American order without important support. Moscow and Washington could start the arduous march to international security and look back to find that no one of consequence was following. The attitude of France is a useful warning that to be effective the consensus must be widened. A successful effort to recover France and also to introduce the Federal Republic of Germany and Japan* into international security institutions is probably basic to their success.

The major difficulty is therefore posed by China. Many elements of international security can be resolved without the participation of the Peking régime: but the armed forces of the United States, the Soviet Union, India, Japan and Australia are unlikely to be altered significantly in arrangements which do not involve China. There are difficulties here which could prove extremely serious. It is possible to conceive of an international order designed, in effect, around China with the object of ensuring that she was contained and deterred in all circumstances. This would be a repetition on a grander scale of the North American–West European security structure designed to deter the Soviet Union. Like N.A.T.O., it could have an internal life of great importance; and the majority of the dangers discussed in Chapter 2 would be, in effect, part of this internal life rather than its external confrontation with China.† Nevertheless, it is a difficult thing

---

* Japan's entry into the C.C.D. is a useful step in this direction. West Germany's leading place in N.A.T.O. has given her what is in present circumstances an even more important part in the management of the world order.

† It is worth noting the extent to which N.A.T.O. through its guarantee structure, has been a force for the disarmament of western Europe. One need only compare the arms levels of NA.T.O. Europe with Sweden or Switzerland. Where nuclear weapons are concerned, Britain's nuclear effort has been reduced on the grounds that it duplicates the Americans; the French *force de frappe* was defeated in the

to conceive unless China becomes actively aggressive; and a military alliance of this kind might well impede a conscious world security order. It would involve the Soviet Government in an exceptionally difficult series of decisions and a more ideologically minded Soviet leadership might at any time decide that an alliance with the West against a Communist state was intolerable. Certainly if Chinese conduct makes it necessary, the rest of the world will respond to apparent dangers; and a united response would create the opportunity to introduce a number of important advances over the present power structure. Ultimately, there could well be a repetition of what the optimists take to be the present evolution of the N.A.T.O.–Warsaw Pact confrontation: namely, that in new days with wiser men the confrontation itself could gradually be turned to a common structure.

An open alliance against China is only likely, however, if there is a general conviction that China has become dangerously aggressive. Only a China which is both belligerent and powerful can be expected to enjoy such an important status. Most major governments now believe that China is defensive in her military outlook; and as long as the main powers adhere to this view there is some basis for working with Peking. A resolution of the problem of China in relation to international security will thus be part of the general evolution of world political life. Judgements cannot be made in general terms. But the Chinese problem is a useful reminder that over a period of time there may well be other revolutionary régimes considering themselves unique and unwilling to go beyond co-existence with the unregenerate world around them. If they are important, the working of international security institutions will become difficult, particularly if the revolution sees itself as a world movement, and is aggressively identified with bodies of supporters in other countries.

It seems reasonable to assume at present that China alone

Assembly on the same grounds; and Germany, Italy, Canada, the Netherlands and Belgium have all had less support for national nuclear weapons than Sweden or Switzerland.

cannot impede the effective consensus needed to work international security institutions provided these enjoy general support elsewhere. She is nevertheless a major exception and imposes limits on how far the international order can go until she can find her full place in it. That place can be prepared by efforts to bring her in on particular arrangements whose political content is not enough to invoke rivalries and whose security content is important enough to attract interest.

The French and Chinese problems illuminate a larger danger. This is the widely held Soviet–American illusion that they are the only powers that really count. There is a real danger that these two will become increasingly preoccupied with their missile forces, their navies, their armoured divisions and their tactical air forces and forget what the roots of power are and the extent to which these are dispersed throughout the world. Virtually the entire American literature of arms control and most of the best contemporary work on strategy dismiss the rest of the world as peripheral. U.S. faces S.U. in a mirror image with great appeal to mathematicians and no doubt to computers. Allies cluster around U.S. at times of decision, some urging her on and some urging compromise. U.S. and S.U. sometimes compete expensively for the formless mass of the third world but more commonly realize that their interests are fundamentally to work together. China stands as a symbol of unreason and uncertainty. Some Americans add a unified and friendly Western Europe as a second U.S. but the mirror image with the Soviets remains surprisingly unchanged. Soviet policy seems to be even more influenced by these notions. The development of a bilateral great power dialogue expresses the joint Soviet–American inability to focus on the many middle and small powers which fill out the world; but it was mainly due to Soviet efforts that Britain and other comparable countries were excluded.

It is possible for Moscow and Washington to imagine that they rule the world only as long as they act with the realism of the Holy Roman Emperors and do not try to exercise their authority. In these circumstances, others may even accept a nominal superiority or even a kind of sovereignty (as so many have done in signing the Charter of the United Nations, with its vast paper powers of enforcement) but they will not allow this to influence their conduct in any significant way. For the substantial objectives of the reform of power, a much broader consensus is indispensable.

In the advance of power and technique, freedom gives way to husbandry. Hunters must become farmers; fishermen must restrict their seasons; housing must be planned; transport must be ordered and licensed. We must abandon old free-ranging habits one by one. So with the development, production, and deployment of arms. We have become too much the masters of nature to be able to rely any longer on its balancing power. We must therefore invent a political régime that will absorb the facts of security as they evolve. This will not be government: and yet security is too fundamental to be an exercise in functionalism. International society has clear and developing interests. Those of its servants who can show that they understand these interests and can represent them could gain the strength to build an adequate world security structure.

INDEX

INDEX